From Both Sides of the Couch

...reflections of a psychoanalyst, daughter, tennis player, and other selves...

BOOKSURGE
AN AMAZON.COM COMPANY

Booksurge, LLC
(An Amazon.com Company)
7290 B Investment Drive
North Charleston, SC 29418

Hardcover copies available by contacting Booksurge at:
customerservice@booksurge.com
(866) 308-6235 extension 5692

Author's note: Names of doctors and patients have been changed
to protect their privacy.

Library of Congress Control Number: 2007902859

Cohen, Fern W.,
From Both Sides of the Couch, reflections of a psychoanalyst,
daughter, tennis player and other selves: a memoir/Fern W. Cohen — 1st ed.

Book Design by Celita Schutz
Text set in Bembo and Peignot
Cover Photograph by Marilynne Herbert
Manufactured in the United States of America

ISBN 1-4196-6441-7

Acknowledgments

This manuscript, born over fifteen years ago as a longish essay that an agent suggested I turn into a book, has had so many incarnations that I cannot begin to thank all those friends, colleagues and family who have supported me along the way—whether through reading, editing, clarifying, questioning or cheering me on—including my patients, past and present, from whom I continue to learn. Among these many, however, a few stand out whom I wish to acknowledge by name:

Melissa Gibson, who read and edited several of the first versions and encouraged me to believe that perhaps I could write something of value for others to read;

Cindy Workman Hyden, whose style, content, and friendship, harken back to the era of Maxwell Perkins, a hands-on editor without peer;

Dr. Steven J. Ellman, without whom I would never have grown into my own voice;

And last but never least, my husband, Dan Cohen. Neither a saint nor a martyr, he has surely had the patience and devotion of each, having read all versions in their many stages over the years, responded to my many questions, reassured and humored me, and tolerated my immersion in this project, which surely at times may have bordered on my neglecting him.

Introduction

Yet another memoir? Well, not exactly.

For all the biographical elements here, my intention has never been to record my own life. Rather, I have tried to convey the defining nature of our earliest relationships and the transformative, at times magical, workings of the process called psychoanalysis.

From childhood we are destined to be shaped by the primary objects in our lives, and in this regard, my relation to my father was no different from any other. But however much the themes might follow a universal developmental path, our own particulars are unique, some mix of constitution, history, and even the serendipitous. When ghosts from childhood haunt us or determine the patterns that constrict us as we go about the business of life, retracing our steps and filtering the primary colors from the mix can become essential toward freeing us to live most fully in the present.

What follows is about my journey to become my own person, a journey that has culminated in my becoming a psychoanalyst, an astonishing yet inevitable outgrowth of my efforts to grapple with the difficulties inherent in growing up as the daughter of a remarkable man, an esteemed jurist who set a standard that seemed impossible to reach. It is also about how and why tennis, almost the sole form of relaxation in the life of a man who was dedicated to his work, initially provided some rare common ground between us—and about how a game became symptom and symptomatic, the playing field on which I would enact some of the profound conflicts of my life. The story begins and ends with tennis; in between is a great deal about the conflicts and dramas of the mind.

Born into my father's universe of unyielding logic and reason, I first had to fall out of his kingdom and then, in the process of picking myself up, discover another language, one that governs how the past and present meet, collide or battle within us—the language of the unconscious, the language of psychoanalysis and my work.

In keeping with this language and characteristic unfolding of a psychoanalytic process, where one wanders back and forth between the present and the past, following the logic of associations and themes, the narrative does not follow a chronological time line. The unconscious is timeless, and if we can relax the bounds of reason and the linear, we can put together the disparate pieces of our personal puzzle in multiple ways and in so doing, find new meaning to familiar people and events.

No one, from Freud on down, has ever claimed that psycho-analysis can cure us of the human condition. Still, in an era of the quick fix, of spin, of massive denial, of mis-attribution, of suppression and repression, I do believe that psychoanalysis has the power to help us to recognize and resolve conflicts that all too often drive us to act in destructive ways. Beyond that, that it can enable us to discover better and more fulfilling compromises. I believe that it is only through our capacity to identify and come to terms with the dark unconscious forces within us that we can free ourselves from the grip of blind and rigid passions to live lives of compassion, creativity, and joy—in our relationships, in our work, and in our play.

Hence, this psychoanalytic tale. It is dedicated with respect, love, and some lingering (if mild) ambivalence toward my father, the late Judge Edward Weinfeld (1901–1988).

CONTENTS

Those who know ghosts tell us that they long to be released from their ghost life and laid to rest as ancestors. As ancestors, they live forth in the present generation, while as ghosts, they are compelled to haunt the present generation with their shadow life.

Hans Loewald, "Therapeutic Action of Psychoanalysis"

mostly about my father

…What thou has inherited from your fathers, acquire it to make it thine and thee…

Freud, quoting Goethe

'*The surprising thing about one's dead,*' Thom Gunn said to me many years ago, '*is that your relationship with them can change over time. Even after they've been dead for years, you still find your feelings about them changing, or growing. And that makes them seem to alter, too.*'

I asked him recently if he still feels that way. 'Yes,' he said. 'Yes. Exactly. The longer people are dead, the more your relationship with them changes.'

Wendy Lesser, **The Amateur**
(1999, Pantheon Books, NY)

The summer that he won his first set of tennis from me, my son Joshua was eighteen or nineteen and I was approaching my fifties. It was a significant milestone for us each—for Josh a sign of growing filial prowess, for me a bittersweet reminder of the galloping passage of time, underscoring as it did that life, especially in one's middle age, is not necessarily about progressing but about coming to terms with finiteness and closure.

To the great relief of my competitive self, that summer was also the one in which Josh took a first set from his father—with the chivalrous disclaimer that the latter had a tennis elbow and his mother was a "head case" so neither win could really qualify as a triumph for him. Never mind. To have held Josh off as long as I did is some indication of the kind of tennis I am capable of playing—on a good day. I have played most of my life and am good enough, at least to have been asked innumerable times if I were a pro, or had ever been ranked. Those questions always induce in me a mix of delight and chagrin, for what strangers don't know and can't see is inside my head and my predisposition to fall apart under pressure, either to double-fault at crucial moments, or worse, to self-destruct from a notable lead.

What I'm really talking about here is the power of the psyche and unconscious mind. Not just mine of course, but the ways in which our unconscious conflicts, identifications and fantasies have the power to determine so much of what we do or don't do, what we can or cannot do, as Freud brought into such sharp focus so long ago. Having undergone a psychoanalysis in my early twenties that transformed the direction of my life, I was well aware that the constellation of internal forces that could undo my best strokes and have me losing games I was more than capable of winning (the symptoms my family and I had long associated with my being a head case on the court) was about something more complex than garden-variety nerves. But during most of those years I was focused primarily on my growing family and evolving professional self and was more or less content to live with whatever psychological weaknesses were embedded in my game. After all, tennis was only a game, a small part of a larger whole at that.

What I didn't realize and would require another psychoanalysis to expose was the degree to which tennis, which I loved from the moment I first stepped on a court, was a link in the chain that bound me to my father, an extraordinary man, whose being was at the center of my mind and at the crux of the major conflicts and anxieties of my life; as one law clerk eulogized him after he died, he was the jurist for whom "good was never good enough, better always the goal." Moreover, for the longest time, I was clueless that my sometime-struggles on the court were indissolubly connected to my efforts to feel competent in my own right as opposed to being the daughter of a man to whom I could never measure up.

As my mid-life psychoanalytic journey evolved, it not only culminated in my becoming my own person but helped me lay the ghost of my father to rest. Not kill him off, I should clarify, but diminish his power to haunt me or infiltrate so much of my life and mind. In the words of the eloquent psychoanalyst Hans Loewald, the process was about converting a ghost into an ancestor, in my case by coming to terms with the differences between my father and me, by mourning, and by allowing the positive to predominate over ambivalence and angry sense of loss. An analysis can do that at its empowering best.

What follows then has to do with psychological bedrock and the ways in which the psychoanalytic process can free us from our personal demons and lay them to rest. By extension, it is also about the nature of our earliest relationships and the extent to which our primary objects, usually our parents, have the power to inform our psychological makeup, to determine our sense of selves and the direction of our lives. In my case, that power resided in my father, whose integrity, sense of moral purpose and unrelenting devotion to work and the power of reason above all else, set a seemingly impossible standard for adult or child to reach.

As someone who occasionally and naively fantasized that only with my father's dying could I come out from under the weight of being his daughter, I miss him more than I could have imagined, less in an immediate personal sense than with an intense longing for the ideals he embodied, especially his integrity and steadfast capacity not to be seduced by personal interest or gain. What you saw was what you got, much to be proud of and to admire. Indeed, I would feel proud to come close to his standards of excellence, just as I would feel grateful to share his capacity for friendship or to be admired (I'll admit) for the quality of my work. But one cannot readily tease apart the individual ingredients that constitute a dynamic whole and so there are major residues of my father in me that I would just as soon have done without. In his lifetime, they may have served him well, but all too often they have been a cross to bear in mine.

A man whose disciplined hold on himself in all areas of his life allowed no room for the play of intense emotions or the power of unconscious mind, my father was "truly a nineteenth century man, born a year too late in 1901…who prided himself on following the dictates of reason and on never having read Freud," as remembered fondly by yet another clerk. And here, I complain. Not because my father held up reason above all else but because he actually seemed proud of his indifference to Freud and his ideas, an astounding position really to hold in the light of Freud's revolutionary impact on our world. Having bypassed college for law school as one could in those days, my father occasionally lamented that he had not gone to college and so was not exposed to a classical education in which tradition Freud surely belongs. However, even after I became drawn in to Freud's universe, first as an adolescent in crisis, then as a professional (teacher, educational therapist, psychologist and psychoanalyst), my father's attitudes about unconscious mind remained unyieldingly the same. Only as an adult did I recognize that his reluctance to cross the familiar boundaries of his world dovetailed with his inability to venture emotionally beyond the reasonable or the conscious known.

It was this characteristic that limited my father's ability to relate to the mind or experience of a growing child. While he had a remarkable intellectual capacity to address the enigmas and complexities that confronted him in his professional life, there was little difference between the private and the public man. That is, my father was inaccessible in a most crucial sense, if one considers some attunement and shared language or experience between parent and child essential, and I do. Because one could have access to him only via his work, my father remained a distant figure whom I could not reach; by the same token, he could not reach me—and why a game comes to figure so dominantly in a narrative about the life of the mind.

It all began when I was around six and accompanied my father on Sunday mornings in spring and summer when he played with George, a former colleague-become-friend, and while they rested between sets, my father would pitch a few balls to me. To this day I can see and feel the six-year-old standing at mid-court facing him, his back to the net, gently pitching the first of a dozen or so balls and telling me when to swing. And swing I did, stepping in to meet the ball with shortened grip on his wooden racquet, far too big for me. From where he stood it would have been hard for me to miss and mostly I did not—but what I remember primarily was the sensation, the ball's brief contact on the strings before it arched away over the net. The excitement was intense, no different from what I feel today when I hit a solid shot, the mix of power and control, the coordination of mind and body when everything is purposeful and without strain. Even weighted down with the too-heavy racquet I didn't feel awkward, and when the ball soared it gave me a brief taste of joy followed by a sense of loss as I returned to the sidelines so my father and George could continue their game.

Whatever else tennis would become for me, those Sunday mornings were a rare opportunity to have my father to myself. But not quite. Although we took the long subway ride together from New York's Lower East Side where we lived up to the courts in the Bronx near Yankee Stadium, there I would lose him to George while I occupied myself on the sidelines, unaware of the frustration I now know I felt as I waited impatiently for the pause-between-sets when it would be my turn. Already struggling with the awesome and distant father whose immersion in his work left him time for little else, by the time I was six, it seemed extraordinary to go off with him alone, an illusion I maintained by focusing on our having left my mother and sister behind at home.

Much as today I recognize my disappointment and anger at having to watch and to wait (having subsequently discovered how hungry, really greedy, I was for more), my dominant memories of that time resonate still with overtones of exhilaration and joy, centered on the closeness to my father so transient and rare. Throughout most of my adult years, I paid scant attention to how little I actually did get to play until our son Josh indignantly drove home the darker side of my pleasure at having received such "crumbs."

Crumbs they may have seemed to Josh who had a sense of self and confidence born of parental availability that I so sorely lacked, but crumbs they were not to me. They were among the links that bound me to my father on those Sunday mornings when my love for tennis became fixed, and tennis became a medium of exchange, a crucible of colliding emotions—from excitement to frustration, from love to hate, from betrayal to revenge—a web of entangled threads that bound me to my father and my past.

Josh was right, of course. For all my suppression and denial, those special moments with my father definitely had their real down sides. For starters, after all these years, waiting to play still fills me with restlessness bordering on anxiety unless I've had my quota for the day. Even pregnancy did not deter me and I must confess with some shame (and perverse pride) that I played tennis into the ninth month of my first one, when the gratification of hitting the ball and working up a sweat offset the recognition of how ridiculous I must look or my anxiety as I rested afterward that I might have hurt the baby. So much so, that once I felt her reassuring movements within, I would swear off playing until after I gave birth, but the next day would dawn and I would yield to temptation again.

Quite irrationally I blamed much of that temptation on my parents who, that summer for the first and only time ever, had rented a house with a tennis court close to the city so my father could commute to work. A court in my own backyard? Watch and wait while others played? Pregnant or not, it was unbearable for me to sit it out and in a family where everyone played, easy enough to rope someone in—especially my sister. Though we both were aware that I was the better player (never openly acknowledged in a family where fairness and doing the best one could were supposed to erase such comparisons), she suggested that we hit just a few, quietly relishing what seemed an unmistakable opportunity to take a set from me. I, of course, took the bait and soon we decided to play just a few games, then why not a set, which an hour later had us tied at twelve-all. At this juncture my father, who usually assumed reason and judgment on everyone's part and so rarely interceded in such matters, came from the house where he'd been working and called a halt—to the best tennis my sister and I did or would ever, play. It was also a striking illustration of my near-delusional state of denial when it came to competition and matters of that ilk.

A quite different instance of that competitive streak arose many years later when my husband and I were playing while Josh and a friend were resting between their sets on the next court. I overheard his friend ask Josh if he beat me, which at the time he hadn't but he answered that he had, an anticipatory lie in keeping with the adolescent necessity of maintaining status and self-esteem with his peers: how could he, a superior athlete, face himself or them if his mother could beat him at tennis? I forgave Josh that fib although I definitely felt deprived of the deference and awe that might have been my due.

Childish, I suppose, as a supposedly mature woman with a full and rich life, yet to have an adolescent male impressed by my prowess at tennis would have been a considerable triumph to me even then. It would have echoed back to my own awkward adolescence when I took refuge in tennis as a safe space where I could hit with the boys and avoid the competition with my slenderer counterparts at the pool. Miserable about the changes that puberty had wrought to my once slim body, I no doubt envied them unconsciously but what I was mostly aware of was contempt: they seemed only to lounge or very occasionally read, mostly non-intellectual stuff at that. I certainly did not perceive that my disdain was a defense against my envy, any more than I saw my dismissal of interest in makeup (confirmed by a vehement declaration to my mother that I had no intention of wearing lipstick until my senior year of high school or maybe beyond) as a defense against my ambivalence about, and intimidation by men.

Hanging out all day at the courts instead of at the pool, I would play for hours with boys my own age or men whose partners hadn't yet showed. (Even pros seemed to enjoy hitting with me and only years later did I realize how much that added to my sense of being different and above the female fray.) Relaxed in the conviction that they were interested in the tennis, not in me, I could play with enough skill and abandon to sustain a hard-hitting rally if not yet a set. It was actually an interesting bit of what analysts call compromise formation: it gave me the sun and the sweat but none of the threat. Although I readily confess to my share of crushes on the local pro or club champion, in my mind it was definitely the game first and the men second, a rationalization of the very first order for sure.

By adolescence I had completely identified with my father's version of the game. Except for the rudiments he learned from his only sister, my favorite aunt who had been on the Hunter College tennis team (a proud bit of family history I can't resist recording here), he was primarily self-taught. Although he looked somewhat awkward and stiff and played with his elbow cramped and close to his body, he was a steady baseline player, a relentless retriever whose joy would have been to keep the ball in play forever. For him to put a ball away at net or any place else bordered on immoral: why would one want to end a rally when the ball was still in play? In fact, he so loved a hard, well-hit shot that he would often drop his racquet to applaud an opponent's beautifully played point; he was equally un-equivocal in deriding a "puffy" shot, his pejorative for any kind of soft ball, be it a drop shot or a slice, whether born of ineptitude or intent. Then too, he played only singles, mistakenly deploring doubles as too slow, having ignorantly dubbed it a "lazy man's game."

Most salient for me about my father's kind of tennis was his global denial of the importance of winning. Indeed, in almost every context of life, he affirmed that doing one's best was the essential thing. Along such lines, his usual response to praise was to comment on the sheer amount of effort and struggle that had gone into a particular opinion or trial, which he reinforced frequently by quoting Thomas Edison who attributed his success to "one-percent

inspiration and ninety-nine percent perspiration." Never did my father seem to manifest any kind of urgency about whether he should
win, certainly not when it came to a game, although in later years
I wondered whether his considerable, if quiet, professional pride in
how rarely his judicial opinions were overturned by an appeals court
represented a kind of winning for sure.

After my father died, I found myself reminiscing with a former law
clerk and tennis player himself who admiringly recalled my father's
love of the game; John went on to insist how very competitively my
father played, driven as he was to do his best. How could he not pur-
sue the game as he did his work? My father did play hard, I agreed,
but what he loved were the sun, the sweat, and the feel of the ball in
play. John persisted and I gave up the debate, in those days being still
in awe of lawyers (my father, of course). But when it came to tennis,
I remained certain: my father might try to live up to some idealized
figures but would not consciously think of competing with any of
them, except perhaps King Gustav of Sweden who played singles
until his nineties, a record my father definitely hoped to best, as he
sometimes reminded us. (After all, he had refused to take senior status
on the bench which would have allowed him to carry a lighter trial load
and instead, he continued to work indomitably until three months
before he died.)

Whatever the other elements, I have no doubt that in the life
of a man whose seriousness, dedication, and sense of purpose were
so exclusively channeled into his work, my father's time on the
tennis court was a respite of unalloyed joy and winning incidental
in the scheme of things. For me, however, it was not, and it was this
conflict—between the self constrained to be like my father and

disavow competition and the one to whom winning became absolutely vital—that became engraved in my version of the game.

Undoubtedly, some of my father's drive was cultural: as the youngest son of hard-working immigrants, he had resolved very early to become a lawyer and pursued his dream single-mindedly, finding no time for stickball, stoop ball, or chasing trolleys, the typical pastimes among boys in his neighborhood in his day. An obedient and dutiful son who grew into a respectful and devoted adult, from what I've gleaned about my father's childhood, it's easy enough to suppose that aggression and competition were suppressed early on. Moreover, knowing as I now do how the roots of our early histories persist, I wonder to what extent my father's lifelong drive facilitated their denial or masked a sense of guilt.

On this subject though, I have many more questions than answers. Did my father ever experience a sense of loss about what he might have missed growing up? What was the impact of the death of his brother Izzy from meningitis on the eve of his Bar Mitzvah when my father was ten? (That story told matter-of-factly, stripped of emotional nuance or implications, then or ever.) And what role did survivor guilt play in the development of the conscientious son who called his parents every day as an adult, who obeyed them when they insisted after his graduation from law school that he turn down a prestigious professional offer to go into an incompatible partnership with his remaining older brother instead, one that ended a scant two years later only upon their father's death?

Whatever the source of my father's tenacious drive, I as a child had no such sense of purpose or direction. Thus whenever I compared myself to him I fell short, lacking something I should have had, and 'lesser than' because my interests did not merge with his. By confusing contrast, being part of his universe engendered a sense of being special, sometimes even better than other children around. For instance, from an early age, my sister and I would often have dinner with our parents after my father came home from work and the subject was usually his day or current events; even the fact that the hour was well past 5:30 or 6:00 when the families around us usually ate distinguished us. We also sat in on the Friday or Saturday evenings of drinks and dinner with my father's friends, many of them prominent or in the public eye themselves, where conversation always centered on politics or the law, all reaffirming for me the sole significance of work and the inferiority of interest in anything else (for me more fodder for shame).

My indefatigable father's priorities ruled outside the house as well: with little room for spontaneity in their lives, my parents went only rarely to theater, movies or concerts, and never to museums. The rare family activity I remember occurred on Sunday evenings as we ate dinner and we usually listened to the radio (and laughed to) the screwy antics of Jack Benny and his sidekick Rochester; indeed, I can hear Benny's wry voice playing off Rochester's gruff rejoinders even now. Otherwise, my father was astoundingly out of touch with matters of everyday life. So much so that midway through a popular musical film that my mother managed one exceptional Sunday afternoon to coax him to see, he leaned over to ask who was that fellow with the very nice voice, referring to Bing Crosby, of whom he had never heard. Barely able to utter Crosby's name, my mother was overcome with such near hysterical laughter that they were almost forced to leave the theater; told at home upon their return, the story immediately became part of amusing family lore. But knowing what I do now about my mother's frustrations with my father, I can't help wondering whether her overreaction was bitter-tinged.

It was my same out-of-touch father who refused to grant a post-ponement of a pretrial hearing that would have required a prime witness to absent himself from the start of spring training. The witness, of whom he again had never heard, was Mickey Mantle. Never shy to acknowledge his ignorance about matters mundane (indeed, possibly proud of it), my father joined in the laughter that erupted in the courtroom when he made his confession—but he remained unimpressed by Mantle's celebrity and decreed that the trial proceed apace.

My father told that story over his relaxing before-dinner-drink, an amusing instance from his day in court. But what came through to me even then was his determination to conduct the kind of fair and expeditious trial for which he rightly became legendary, along with his quiet pride that he had not been seduced into bending the rules. And while I shared that pride, my feelings were curiously mixed. Although I was not at all interested in baseball (not surprising in a family where tennis was the only sport that counted), I certainly knew who Mantle was and felt strangely tantalized to learn that he would appear before my father. At the same time I felt oddly ashamed of my longing to be touched by fame.

Normally of course, it is just such distant popular heros who safely stir the adolescent's desires and dreams. But the figure of awe lived in our household and his were the standards I internalized;

anything other felt unworthy and instilled guilt and shame. These were among the wellsprings of the patterns I would play out over and again on the court, where, given an opportunity, however fleeting, to share common ground with my father, tennis took hold.

In actuality, our tennis outings were few and far between and ended by the time I went off to sleep-away camp, just turned seven and far too young. We must have rallied or played an occasional set later but never regularly, not even when my game was equal to or surpassed his. There's no dramatic reason for this other than the Spartan amount of time my father allotted for play and the ridiculous early hours he kept, against which by adolescence I managed to rebel. (In later years, his tennis-playing law clerks would semi-cheerfully meet him at whatever courts opened early enough to suit his insomnia and work habits.) Still, the hold of tennis on my life became a sustaining organizing force, a constant among the zigs and zags, central to who I am and how I feel about myself.

As I've wrestled with my very conflicted relationship to and with my father, my game, along with so much else in my life began to change, from the inside out, so to speak. Among many unexpected outcomes, about this I was to be delightfully surprised. For years I used to complain that by the time my head was in the right place, my body would have fallen apart but as the decades have passed, the gap between mind and body has narrowed and amazingly, I have actually experienced a sense of progress rather than despair. (I do, however, rue the inability of the psychoanalytic process to banish the aching joints that make it harder now to reach a ball on the far side of the court.)

Over the years my game has continued to grow, and in the more recent past I have finally come into my own as a player, a derivative of the struggle to become my own person that is much of what my life has been about. Indeed, it has taken me much of a lifetime to recognize the complexity of the forces set in motion when I step on a court to play, a Gordian knot that has mind lagging far behind body when it comes to change. Unaware until my twenties that such forces existed, I believed with my father that playing tennis was a function of learning ground strokes and acquiring mastery through practice and hard work.

So work at it I did. Fueled by my passionate young attachment to my father I quickly acquired the essential tools, although no one, I least of all, recognized the quality of desperation generated by that attachment and my urgency to close the distance between him and me. One early indication: it rained on the day I was scheduled to have my first formal lesson up at those courts in the Bronx where my father had pitched those few balls to me and I was near inconsolable at the delay, despite reassurances that the lesson was only being postponed until the following week.

Naturally, some shots were harder to learn than others. I particularly remember the struggle to learn a backhand and my intermittent despair that I might not. It was almost as an afterthought (or possibly desperation) near the end of a lesson that prompted a pro to suggest that I bring my racquet back with two hands to take the weight off my arm but to swing through only with one. Much to my relief and delight, coordinating those motions left me with a strong and graceful backhand that has remained basically unchanged to this day. Unorthodox then (except for the colorful Pancho Segura), it tends to look two-handed and onlookers often assume that it is. But it's not and it doesn't matter whether it is or isn't—I love it. It's my best shot and I can drive it down the line or cross court on the run with a sense of control and power that epitomizes for me the joy of playing. It is the same feeling I experience when the rest of my game is on—my version of a state of grace—some finely tuned balance of internal and external that allows me to be assertive and unworried, capable of deep pleasure in victory or defeat.

That feeling about my backhand is more or less constant. No matter how I struggled to learn it or perhaps because I did, it has empowered me, instilling a confidence that allows me to accept an error as just that instead of seeing it as a sign of imperfection in myself, a proclivity to which I was so long vulnerable. That confidence is not unlike the sense of security a small child develops in relation to what the great British pediatrician-turned-psychoanalyst Donald Winnicott suggested the *good-enough* mother provides: she who is available to meet both physical and emotional needs, who is able to tolerate the different moods and experiences of infancy or childhood, who can hold or comfort, indulge or set limits, and who in the process conveys that she will be dependably attuned and available—enough of the time.

This is not to say that the good-enough mother doesn't occasionally get angry, impatient, or even fail her child, but rather to stress that she provides the wherewithal for herself and the child, singly or together, to survive interference or discord and regroup from whatever emotional or physical slights might have occurred. But survive or regroup is what I often could not do on the tennis court. Despite the constancy of my backhand, my psyche, fueled by my propensity to react disproportionately to the matters at hand, tended to kick in, having early on seized the game as a field for playing out the conflicted parts of myself. In other words, my capacities as a player were inextricably interwoven with my sense of self and self-esteem, rendering body and mind exquisitely sensitive to injuries and slights and variously over-reactive or under-assertive to the realities at hand. But since when do conscious will and intent have control over un-conscious body and mind?

Which brings me, inescapably, to Freud—for just as my father pervaded my growing up, so Freud informs my adult self. I am referring, of course, to psychoanalysis, especially to my own experiences on the couch, where the most valuable learning about self and other can occur. Without doubt, it was psychoanalysis that helped me distinguish and separate my father's admirable and legendary qualities from those that had a negative impact on me. It also led to my evolution as a psychologist and somewhat long overdue decision to become a psychoanalyst myself; it led me also to my analyst Dr. Stevenson, the most immediate among the links that connect me so profoundly to Freud. (Why I never thought about becoming an analyst sooner has to do with my seeing my own analysts as "the ones who knew" and courtesy of transference, ceding to them the authority that belonged to my father—and emphatically not to me.)

There is a beautiful irony in the fact that the men who have so shaped my sense of self, my father and Freud, shared a dedication to work and a rare kind of integrity and discipline but were so opposite from one another in one essential—the role of reason. My father was the ultimate rational man: he believed that one could find a steady and creative course in life through reason and logic, as clearly he did. Freud, by contrast, was an explorer of the unknown, who mapped the mind and introduced us to its dynamics as the creator of psychoanalysis, the process that evolved from such seemingly nonrational matters as hysteria and dreams. His work was unified by his conviction that the forces of the unconscious—the efforts we all make to protect ourselves against our conflicts or impulses, whether through repression, denial or undoing (to mention only a few weapons in our arsenal of defenses)—are surely more powerful than the forces of reason and intellect to which my father subscribed.

Not that Freud did not believe in reason or my father in the unconscious but that their perspectives were vastly different. In particular, my father's acknowledgment of the unconscious seemed more perfunctory than real. Without a doubt, coming to terms with this monumental limitation on his part and its influence on me has driven much of what I have done or achieved, beginning when I was away at college and forced to confront what seemed the apparently irreconcilable differences between us. It was that confrontation that led me ultimately to embrace the enormity of the invisible and unconscious forces in my own and others' lives.

But growing up under the man who set a near impossible standard to reach, whose unimpeachable being took on the awesome power of commandment, I was a long way from any kind of conception of unconscious mind. Why I didn't or couldn't take a more rebellious course as a growing child surely had to do with (in addition to constitution and other imponderables) the utter absence of conflict or anger in the household. The consistency of polite, everyday discourse and behavior (*please, thank-you* and *may I* at all the appropriate times) reigned between and among us all, child or adult. My parents never argued or raised their voices to us or one another and they openly disapproved of the shouting or yelling that some-times came from apartments around us while their behavior made it clear that *we* didn't do that kind of thing.

With a single exception that occurred when I was around nine or ten: one evening as my parents were getting dressed to go out to some event, I heard my father complain irately to my mother about a recently arrived order of bow ties, his one clothing indulgence. (He had a collection of over one hundred which he proudly tied himself.) There was something wrong with this batch, my father insisted and my mother denied as they went back and forth in ag-grieved tones about the size or the shape, I don't remember which. What I do remember is my shock about their 'fighting' and the tears of panic that set in almost immediately after they gave us their usual good-night kisses and left the house: I was convinced there was going to be a divorce. My aunt (our usual baby sitter) had also gone out that evening and it was my sister, then around thirteen, who took her place. But even she, to whom I also went for comfort or reassurance, was unable to calm me down and had to call my aunt back from a neighbor's house. The next morning my mother and father smilingly reassured me that nothing was wrong and the episode quickly lost its charge—or so we all assumed.

Early on I had internalized a model with no room for aggression. As I grew, its manifestations seemed dangerous beyond the pale: my panic of that night, like my despair when my tennis lesson was canceled, was an unidentified harbinger of how ill-equipped I was to cope with intense emotions, let alone conflict or anger in any form. Moreover, each of the few times I risked going against the prevailing order as a child, the consequences conveyed unmistakably that one did not defy or rebel: punishment was swift and severe. For instance, upon my innocent experiment as a six or seven year old with a swear word directed at Fred, the man who delivered our clean laundry each week, my mother promptly washed out my mouth with soap—no questions asked; in our family, no one ever swore. The fact that I can count on the fingers of one hand my few excursions into rebellion of any sort indicates how early I must have learned to suppress anger and dissent. By the time I was an adolescent, I simply lacked the tools to do otherwise.

While I've never been able to recapture exactly what I did say that morning to Fred, whom I liked and who invariably greeted me with a friendly smile, I am certain that my swearing had nothing to do with him. He was dark like my father and about the same age, so it seems likely to me now that my swearing at him was a displacement of something intended for my father instead. But that childish experimentation paled beside a much more serious expression of complicated rage toward my father that took place one morning after he had shaved and showered.

Part of a ritual, I would frequently watch him in the bathroom as, towel wrapped around his waist, he prepared a frothy lather in a wooden bowl, next applied the foam with a beautiful ivory-handled brush and then shave; sometimes he would even let me make the lather myself. Afterward he would shower as I waited to hand him his towel when he emerged. But one morning I varied the routine: seized by an imp of the perverse (which I understood nothing about), I threw the towel on the floor instead of handing it to him. The punishment was immediate and absolute—I was barred forever from the bathroom without any discussion of what might have prompted my behavior. More important, I lost what was supposed to have been a benign exchange between parent and child.

Except, of course, it wasn't benign at all. My parents must have been completely unaware of how provocative and frustrating it was for me to watch as my father emerged nude from the shower. I'm not sure who initiated these misguided sessions, later described as an opportunity to introduce me to male anatomy, but they lasted long enough for me to imbue them with multiple meanings (sexual and other), connected to a special time with my father (sexual and other). What with the drama of waiting already in place (the pause between sets for my turn), it seems likely that my impatience at being on the sidelines again, mightily compounded by the matter of the over-stimulation of looking at the penis I could not touch, provoked me to throw down the towel in angry protest.

(A significant experience in and of itself, the ritual of holding the towel in the bathroom for my father dovetailed with an even more charged experience of over-stimulation and frustration of much longer duration—that of my sleeping in the kingdom of the untouchable father and the mother who shared his bed—about which, more to follow further on.)

But the incident that undoubtedly must have inhibited all further overt defiance on my part occurred one Sunday morning when I was around seven and went to visit with my mother as she awoke and she sleepily asked what my sister and I had done the day before when my aunt had been baby-sitting for us. Full of early morning chatter, I happily replied that we had gone to the movies and was about to tell her what we had seen.

Suddenly alert, "I thought you were going ice-skating," my mother said, to which I accurately replied that ice-skating hadn't even come up as an option *that* day although it had been one of the alternative plans my mother and my aunt had originally discussed. To this day it's quite clear to me that we (my sister, my aunt and I) chose the movies that Saturday by tacit agreement, which is what I told my mother who kept maintaining that I was not telling the truth. In fact, unless I was prepared to admit that I was lying (about whether ice-skating had come up on the actual day), I would be punished for my crime.

Semantics or my mother's interpretation versus my literal recounting, whatever, I soon found myself enveloped in a round of irrationality throughout which my mother kept insisting that I must acknowledge that I had lied. That, of course, I could and would not do. Had I not grown up in a household where reason and justice were the law of the land? Surely truth and fairness would out, so I stuck to my version of the events, unwilling to believe that I had committed a punishable offense. No matter. I was to be kept back from the singular treat my father had planned for my sister and me and which I had been anticipating for days—a subway expedition, a ferry ride to the Statue of Liberty, a climb to the top and then back home.

But what followed was worse: the man who prided himself on

listening to all sides of an argument in order to come up with a fair and objective assessment of events was nowhere to be found. Instead, my father accepted my mother's version de facto, basically abandoning me to her logic whereby I would have to admit to a crime I hadn't committed if I wanted to avoid being punished; this I continued to refuse to do. So he and my sister went off leaving me desolate behind. It was a double-header of betrayal, by my mother, then by my father, of his ideals, and of me.

Although my basic perspective on the matter has not changed, it has broadened over the years, especially with respect to my mother's role and the probability that her unconscious envy and anger at my father (who was, after all, leaving her behind) might have prompted what today I see as a displaced attack on me. But whatever the backdrop of that memory of compound betrayal and abandonment, public history reinforced my private drama: when my father and sister returned home, it was to the news that the Japanese had bombed Pearl Harbor and the country was at war; thus were both events forever conflated in my mind. (Old enough to be shocked by the outbreak of war, I also felt curiously soothed by the correspondence of my own disaster to that which occurred to the nation at large.)

I'm not sure whether I was more wounded by my mother's surprise attack or by my father's failure to intervene but the cataclysm undoubtedly overturned my world, at least when it came to anger and trust. While it was years before I was able to wonder why my judicious father should have sided so completely with my mother, his behavior confirmed my sense of danger lest I might, unsuspecting, break a rule; beyond that, it sealed my anger underground.

(Half a lifetime later, when I was teaching a college class on developmental tasks of childhood and adolescence and trying to enliven a discussion of the oedipal triangle, I switched gears and asked my rather passive students what it might be in several of the fairy tales we had just read, that led the fathers to abandon their children (often their daughters) to the treachery of the wicked stepmothers. Or in my actual words, why "the fathers tended to be such wimps." After a very long silence, a deep voice from the back of the room boomed out, "Slam, bam, thank-you ma'am," encapsulating the sexual component to the answer, and possibly also explaining why my father abandoned me to my mother's attack. Naturally, I knew nothing about such matters when I was seven.

I suppose some might think my experience of betrayal by my father might have tipped some internal scale that would have allowed me to recognize imperfection in, or generate some anger toward him, but my awe and denial were already too well in place for that. And as I got older, internal pressures to do my best continued to keep me in line. By the time I was in high school and my father was appointed to the bench, it was simply inconceivable to harbor negative feelings toward the man Justice Brennan of the Supreme Court would extol as, "a man whose life commands attention and devotion from every corner of the legal profession… a judge who personifies the majesty of the bar." It wasn't long before I transferred much of my awe to other men of stature in their fields, inevitably and most powerfully to my analysts, especially Dr. Stevenson, who had been recommended as "the best" by a supervisor and analyst I greatly admired.

But I have gotten ahead of the extremely naive player I was when my version of tennis was based on my father's, which he learned in the era of amateur status when the strokes and rules of decorum pervaded the atmosphere with a kind of civility and grace long since gone. That was when whites were *de rigueur,* when crowds were pin-drop silent and applauded politely only at the end of a point or game, when winning was about becoming a champion in a more olym-pian sense of the word. Tennis was a gentlemanly game, definitely not about grandstanding or meteors that flash and disappear, a game modulated by tonality and the steady rhythm of a Haydn or Bach, not the atonality of a Schoenberg or the percussive beat of rock.

When it came to change, my father—who usually settled matters of opinion or taste with a philosophical shrug and the sonorous admonition *de gustibus non disputandum est* (about matters of taste there can be no argument)—seemed unable to follow his own rule. Uncomfortable with the new or the unfamiliar, he remained loyal, even locked in to his version of the game, too often focused on a particular tree instead of the overall surround. Hence, he was dis-missive of Connors's pumping up, disapproving of Agassi's hippy hair and droopy shorts, appalled by the tantrums of McEnroe. (Nor is it a leap for me to script his scornful intonations on the matter of Venus Williams's rhinestone-studded black outfit and matching boots at the US Open, 2004.)

Beyond that, my father's attitude created a rigidity that interfered with his ability to appreciate, let alone enjoy, the kinds of characters and events from which the incremental stuff of growth and develop-ment occur—the exuberant landmark challenge match of the sexes between Billie Jean King and Bobbie Riggs, the superb controlled turbulence of Navratilova or the transformation of Agassi from mercurial adolescent to man of persistence and will. Certainly it was not happenstance that my father continued to play with his wooden racquet way into the era of the metal and only yielded on the orders of his doctor when a bad shoulder left him with no choice. Change was alien, if not anathema to him.

Above all else, he played tennis as he conducted the rest of his life. Unfailingly polite to all with whom he came in contact, whether taxi driver, security guard at the courthouse or Justice of the Supreme Court, he did not attack, from anger or anything else; any aggression he may have felt was under wraps. As Justice Thurgood Marshall made a point of saying at a memorial service for him at the Federal Courthouse several months after he died (in gentle Southern mellifluous drawl), "…take it from me, wherever you go in the country (bar association, legal or judicial conference), anybody that mentions Eddie mentions that he never, never, never said anything bad about anybody." No doubt about it, on or off the court, my father was a hard act to follow.

He also almost never swore—except for the very very infrequent "damn" or still rarer "hell and damnation" occasioned when he missed a shot on the court. But even those expostulations lacked the quality of expletive and were mild expressions of amused frustration directed against himself. I, on the other hand, do swear, undoubtedly in reaction to the prohibition. I began in late adolescence, first on the tennis court as a bit of self-definition and assertion that never did die away. It's not excessive and while I'm not exactly proud of this 'developmental achievement,' I am aware of its utility for me since it does release some anger that otherwise might be turned within. (In fact, the first time I explode with an expletive after a poor shot in early spring, my husband announces that the season has started for real.)

Although I have no doubts about my father's inability to relate to the raw, sometimes demonic power of competition that can lead some to self-destruct, sometimes I wonder whether his denial of the importance of winning was in aid of bolstering his non-aggressive stance. But I am confident that his admiration for those he idealized did not leave him much room for overt competition or for its toxic cousin envy. Against such forces he was well-defended and I am convinced he was unaware that they might exist within him. Indeed, although he often repeated that he felt he had lived his life to the fullest, I believe that some of his unrelenting involvement with work had a large component of warding off and defending against feelings—not an uncommon solution among people who fear being overwhelmed by potentially intense emotions. Not surprisingly, similar deficits applied to me.

If I were to compare the game of tennis that I inherited from my father to the contemporary one, its transformation seems remarkably analogous to the evolution that psychoanalysis has undergone since Freud. In each, the frame, the vocabulary and the ground rules have remained basically the same but the process and the focus have shifted dramatically. Tennis today is characterized by a much more aggressive level of play, greater emphasis on physical fitness (*viz.*, the over-100 mph serves), the tie-breaker and much less formality on both sides of the court. So too is psychoanalysis now radically different from the authoritarian process that took hold in the first generations after Freud.

Back then it was a decidedly one-way system in which the blank-screen analyst made interpretations about transference or resistance to the patient, especially in America in the fifties and sixties when it was carried to austere and impersonal extremes. These days, by contrast, the analyst acknowledges his or her role in the analytic pair and uses it to important effect. The shift in psychoanalysis has been seismic, and I, by sheer happenstance of timing, have been privileged to benefit from both its classic and contemporary incarnations. While my first analyses dated from the heyday of austerity, my more recent one occurred as analysts were acknowledging their subjectivity and conceptually speaking, analyst and analysand had become a *we*.

As a relative newcomer to the profession, I welcome the changes that have accrued to psychoanalysis and at the same time find myself filled with admiration for the expansive foundation Freud laid with its built-in potential for change and growth. It seems to me that the present retains a strong yet flexible tie to the past and I like to think that Freud would appreciate what has evolved. (Perhaps it's not too fanciful to suggest that the foundation is similar to that of our Constitution whose elastic "necessary and proper" clause allows for flexibility and change.) Although Freud could be authoritarian toward those who wanted to reject some crucial aspect of theory (Jung, for example, who would not accept sexuality, infantile or otherwise as at the core of the psyche and development), he was remarkably open to change in the larger scheme of his thinking. Not only did he challenge the narrow sexual mores of his time, he often turned conventional wisdom on its head. This was certainly the case when it came to decoding dreams or understanding hysterics who until then were considered constitutionally degenerate and therefore untreatable by those in the medical field.

Except for Josef Breuer, the prominent Viennese physician who first stumbled on the effectiveness of hypnosis with his patient Anna O when he discovered that the sometimes lurid symptoms of hysterics had unconscious meaning, usually about some sexual conflict that had been repressed. But while Breuer (whose lead Freud would follow) became intimidated by Anna O's hysterical pregnancy (derived from her fantasy that he was the father) and discharged her in panic as 'cured,' Freud stayed the course with his own patients. It was not long before he began to recognize the limitations of hypnosis and abandoned it in favor of free association as a more effective tool to access unconscious mind.

Even more significant and consistent with Freud's uncanny ability—genius really—to conceptualize what others could not, he had begun to recognize the dynamics of transference which Breuer had not. It was transference that had made Anna O fall in love with Breuer and fantasize her pregnancy with his child, just as it was transference to Freud as her father that prompted Dora, Freud's adolescent patient, to break off her treatment with him as a form of revenge. It was also Freud's genius (not to mention his capacity for humor) that allowed him to see that it was again transference and not his personal charm that was inducing his women patients to fall in love with him. But possibly I idealize Freud in my quest to have a more accepting model than my father who was so lacking in the light touch and remained so unyielding to change.

So perhaps it's not surprising that when it comes to tennis, in contrast to my respect and admiration for the developmental shifts that have occurred within psychoanalysis over the years, I find myself caught someplace between tremendous appreciation for the positive developments and a bittersweet sense of loss, colored of course by the resonance of my childhood and my past. For me that game remains epitomized by a match between Frank Parker and Jack Kramer in the finals of the US Open then at Forest Hills, when the tie-breaker was yet to come and tennis was still a strictly amateur sport.

On a quiet Sunday morning, my sister and I climbed to the top of the sedate stadium we had reached by subway and a walk through tree-lined streets to watch the two white-clad men play it out—with long rallies from the baseline and solid returnable serves that seemed indistinguishable from one another until the set was tied at 22-or 23-all. Even the tension got a little boring but I didn't mind because I had a crush on Parker and took secret pleasure in watching his handsome serious face as he kept the ball in play. (I didn't understand why I preferred him to Kramer who was handsome in his blond way and played just as well—in this instance better, since he eventually won the match. Now I realize that Parker's dark, lean intensity reminded me of my father, a displacement of feelings I knew nothing about at the time.)

I still remember my guilty sense of dismay when Kramer won, and my dismay at my dismay; imbued already as I was with my father's golden rule about doing the best one could, how could I fathom my passionate desire for Parker to win? Or my intense disappointment when he did not, since he had done his best and that was all that mattered. Or was it? Clearly, nothing in the climate of my childhood had prepared me for either crushes or the vicissitudes of play in the real world, where competition was part of the fundamental order of the universe and took precedence over doing the best one could.

Freud has written that the hallmark of a mature and healthy adult is his capacity to work and to love; others have since inferred the inclusion of the capacity for play—to develop hobbies, to explore other worlds (through drama, literature, music, art), to create, and to fantasize. For the child, play is crucial, the means by which he or she learns to negotiate the world: a form of trial action, it can provide an opportunity to attain mastery, to identify with loved figures, to take safe revenge on hated ones, to turn passive into active and to fantasize, whether for coping, comfort, encouragement or repair. From play stems the wherewithal to experiment, to risk the unknown, to have a sense of humor, all of which my father lacked both as child and adult—as did I.

Only once did I know him to lose himself in something so mundane as play and by then I was an adult myself. It occurred one weekend during a family gathering at our country home when we decided to play a rare set of doubles as the sun went down, bantering jocularly as we paired my husband and my sister against my father and me. At first the play was straightforward but as the afternoon waned the mood became giddy and the warfare began: toward the end of the second set in which my father and I were slightly ahead, he and I called a ball out. "Impossible," my husband and sister shot back. From their side, they insisted, they could see that the ball had been in. My father and I pointed to the mark; clearly the evidence was on our side.

But my husband (*agent provocateur*) and sister became adamant, undoubtedly reacting to the vehemence with which my father and I resisted and took off on a provocative roll, caught up in the prospect of proving a bias on the part of the man who so prided himself on his capacity to be objective and fair. Dared they suggest we had cheated to make the point? But my father and I stood firm, happily shored up by one another, and soon the court became a playground with kids challenging kids for turf, each side unbudging in the rightness of its position. I loved it all—challenged on this court, my father became one of us in a moment of play.

Had I learned to play or identified with someone other than my father, I'm fairly certain that the tennis court would not have become such a forum for enacting the primary issues of my life. Moreover, it's clear to me now that my father's inhibition regarding play in almost any of its forms severely limited his ability to put himself in another's place or imagine himself in other roles; it certainly contributed to keeping him far removed from what was going on in everyday life. To bridge the distance, one had to speak his language and enter his world and for the longest time I tried, even though it meant pushing aside what interests I had for his.

Have I mentioned yet that my father loved to walk and walked to and from work, at least until he moved uptown, and sometimes even then? Or that his favorite lunch-time break during the week was to walk across the Brooklyn Bridge and back, but not before he ritually touched the pole on the far side? Or that on Sundays, regardless of season, he usually set out for a brisk walk from Third Street to Fifty-Ninth and Fifth and then back again for a very, very, very dry martini with a twist of lemon (the vermouth just passed over the glass) before his lunch and then a nap?

When I was around eleven or twelve, seizing upon the walks as an opportunity to spend time with him, although I didn't yet much like walking, I began occasionally to accompany him on those Sunday morning treks. I asked questions about his work and received answers about a trial or the complexities of the law that I usually didn't understand but kept the conversation going as if I did. For years I assumed that my inability to comprehend such matters, like the foggy feeling I got reading some political or legal article in the newspaper, meant I wasn't smart enough—until I learned that not understanding can be an aggressive defense, a way of shutting someone or something out.

One day, when I was around thirteen, intrigued by what I'd heard about Greenwich Village where I'd never been although we lived only a mile or so away, I asked my father to vary his route and he affably agreed. But once there he seemed out of place, uncomfortable with the unfamiliar streets. And I was uncomfortable too, awkward and unknowingly guilty for having enticed him to break a habit which he rarely did, not even with my mother who also occasionally took those Sunday walks with him. Of course, my guilt was compounded by having taken her place (in my mind, winning out over her). But whether the discomfort was mutual or only mine projected into him, my father did not seem to enjoy looking in the windows of the galleries and shops we passed and could not point out landmarks or talk about Village history. So the excursion initiated out of excited curiosity turned to disappointment and persuaded me that I never could close the distance between him and me. Eventually

I gave up trying and created further distance on my own.

This is not to say that I didn't try to talk to my father about what was going on in my life—that I loved learning French (which pleased him I'm sure), that the clouds of stinking sulphured smoke from a failed chemistry experiment at my new school had driven us laughingly from the lab the previous day (which amused him), that I was feeling stumped about a short story I had been assigned to write (which might have concerned him). But my efforts to draw him in seemed to fail and conversations were closed circles: they went back to his neutrally reassuring "do the best you can," or to his work. At some point, that was not enough for me, while doing my best became too much. It would be years before I realized how that failure might be related to lapses or incapacities on his part, not mine, as I had always assumed.

If a parent cannot pay attention to who a child is or what she does, cannot share enough of a basic vocabulary, irrespective of his or her actual successes or accomplishments, that child may internalize a lasting sense of unimportance and insignificance in the scheme of things. Coming to terms with this profound limitation of my father and its consequences for me has been a constant through much of what I have done or achieved. At the same time, it has etched in sharp relief how the singular bridge between us, the near halcyon moment when a father fondly pitched a few balls to his six-year-old daughter, can have so anchored itself in me and so readily transmuted into a staging area and battleground for the core conflicts of my life.

To some players, a drop shot is a drop shot is a drop shot. But for me it became the essence of male power (acquired through my father), to make me feel helpless and inconsequential. On balance,

I cannot say whether the power of men, so painfully impressed upon me by my father's unwitting distance and total preoccupation with work, has been only a negative force in my life. Admittedly, the cost has been great, to the extent that I have battled much of my life with feeling inadequate and forever outside the realm of men. However, that competition also became a proving ground that left me with skills and competence that I would not have dared to believe were mine, even if at times, I have had to give it all away with a double fault at set-point.

The first intimation that tennis might be about more than sun and sweat and ground strokes occurred one summer at camp when I ended up in the finals of the tennis tournament playing against Ronnie, my bunkmate and best friend. The tournament was part of Color War, a ten-day climax at the otherwise non-competitive camp my parents had chosen in keeping with the family ethic that learning was more important than winning and sports were about having fun. As the culmination of the summer, Color War heightened everyone's natural desire to win and definitely legitimized mine; I threw myself into the fray with a ferocity that surprised me, unknowingly con-flating my very real competitive instincts with my responsibilities as captain of the Blue Team.

In like fashion, I also tried to ignore the uneasy feelings of rivalry and ambiguity occasioned by the fact that Ronnie was captain of the Green Team; already in my mind she could be either friend or foe but not both. From the start I was aware of some tension but attributed it only to our very different styles: I was always exhorting my team members to push themselves as if every game or event mattered to the utmost; Ronnie was smiling and relaxed, and encouraged her team gently as though she would like them to try but didn't mind that much if they didn't win. Her attitude puzzled me since I didn't believe it was possible to do well unless one did one's best, and that, I had already defined as mandating limitless struggle and effort. When it came to tennis, not only had I put in much more practice-time, my strokes were better than hers. Thus as we began, I felt primed to win especially in the face of Ronnie's apparent nonchalance, my excite-ment and confidence buttressed by the passion to win I had adopted as captain of a team.

What followed was a rude awakening to the life of the mind. While I have no memory of the specifics of the match (a lacuna reflecting the nature of my game, then totally lacking in strategy or psychological warfare), to this day, I can conjure up the sense of incredulity-bordering-on-panic that set in when I found myself behind 5-2 in the second set, at love-forty, facing Ronnie, who was about to serve for the match with a cushion no less—of three match points. How did I get there? How had it happened that I was now facing certain loss to an opponent whose weak backhand, unpolished strokes and apparent lack of effort (which I had taken to be indif-ference), had brought me point by point to this moment where she seemed about to win? How could she win when she'd never even appeared to care about tennis except when it had been an assigned activity of the day? How could I lose when I had spent so much more time practicing and clearly loved the game more than she?

These were the disorganizing thoughts that multiplied in frequency and intensity as my disbelief turned to recognition of the galloping momentum over which I seemed to have no control. And worse, the harder I tried, the less effective I became. Then followed heart-pounding agitation, despair at the prospect of losing and what I now realize can only have been hate-unto-rage. But at the time (and for years afterward) I could not identify that last, nor even consider the possibility that so intense a feeling as hate might be directed against a friend, let alone a best friend.

So, courtesy of the resourceful mental gymnastics of which a desperate psyche is capable, I turned the onslaught of escalating unfamiliar emotions against myself and attributed everything to my inadequate playing, that is, to my inadequate self. My chaotic feelings were no longer related to the person who was about to be the cause of my defeat (Ronnie), but took shape as a deep sense of self-loathing I had never experienced before. As I would discover only more than half my lifetime later with Dr. Stevenson, this derived from a very diminished sense of self and why losing so often for me became equated with being never good enough.

I was also dimly aware that Ronnie had driven a wedge into the order of my universe, in particular the sense of safety and specialness that went with being my father's daughter and its corollary, the fairness of things if one does one's best. No way could I know that the dynamics stirred that day would galvanize an arsenal of defenses and rationalizations going forward as I sought to deny the panoply of underlying conflicts and emotions the match had set off, especially the emergence of the competitive and aggressive parts of myself. Although it would be years before I could identify and acknowledge them, these contained the power to undo me and make me lose hold of myself, that is, of my good-enough sense of self, which for years tended to vanish whenever I faced the prospect of diminishing loss. Time and again they would convert into demons fighting a battle of my own making, then morph into fury and panic that rendered me vulnerable, helpless to defend myself assertively, let alone to win.

To get back to Color War: just as I can't describe how I got to triple-match-point in the finals, I can't say how I quelled the heart-pounding agitation to work my way, point by point, back from the edge of the precipice to win that game, the next, and finally the set. But not the match. We were well into the third set with my lead of 5-4 when it began to rain and play was postponed until the next day: that's when I went on to lose that set and with it the match. Yet however strong my disappointment at the loss, it paled in comparison to the violent feelings that had erupted the previous day. I may have managed to dig down into some reservoir to pull myself back from a humiliating defeat but I had also uncovered my own San Andreas fault which I wouldn't identify for decades to come: suppressing aggression and competition as part of myself. It also signaled the eventual necessity of psychological separation from and disidentifca-tion with, a father whose austerity proscribed emotional excesses in any shape or form.

Over the years, negotiating the shoals of that constellation would require me to tease apart the unconscious strands of assertion and aggression that were hopelessly confounded in my mind, where to sustain enough aggressive energy to drive home a victory was to balance on a tightrope from which I too readily could fall off. It hurts to fall, and when I did, I too easily got caught up in the humiliation of the cuts and bruises instead of staying focused on the task at hand; hence, all too often I blew away a winning edge.

Ideally of course, it would be better neither to swallow one's anger nor to explode with it, but to maintain a good-enough balance between the two requires a capacity to accept one's aggression as well as emotional freedom from feared retaliation for one's fantasied deeds. It's a difficult balance for some of us to reach. We all have hate or the potential for it in us and that, I believe, my father did not understand, at least when it came to raising children. ("You don't hate," he would correct my sister or me with a serious smile at the dinner table to some spontaneous expostulation about a friend or a thing, "you might dislike intensely" instead. Hate, he implied, was too strong and we should be able, by virtue of reason and being reasonable, to control it.)

By no means however, is this an apologia for acting out our hate. But to deny its existence leaves us vulnerable to having to ward it off, to expending enormous energy to keep it at bay, and to suffering from anxiety along the way in its stead. Unless or until we come to terms with our aggressive selves, hate and anger can rob us of the wherewithal to love, to work and to play and of their correlates, fulfillment, creativity and joy.

Alas, there is no easy formula for finding the balance between assertion and sufficient aggressive energy to compete without being afraid of one's power to hurt and destroy. Sorting these elements, uncovering ancient fantasies and defusing old conflicts can be a task suitable for a psychoanalysis. When the aggression embedded in those unconscious fantasies is recognized and worked through, in the language of the trade, it becomes neutralized.

Mine, however, for so long was not. In truth, and very much in hindsight, I was afraid of my power and the damage I might do; I was afraid of retaliation too. If I put away, smashed or otherwise aggressively rendered my opposition helpless, surely the loss would provoke the same humiliated fury in him or her that it sometimes stirred in me. (That, by the way, is a prime example of a projection, in which one puts one's feelings or fears into someone else. It's like looking into a mirror and seeing only oneself.)

Obviously, the threshold for coping with the pressures of competition can vary enormously from person to person and time to time. Nowadays, more and more frequently, I can and do pick myself up just as many people do most of the time. In which context, John McEnroe comes to mind: in his exquisite championship days when he could do no wrong, his angry explosions seemed to work for him; at some point they no longer did and detracted from his game, it seems to me, perhaps an example of aggression gone awry.

Closer to home, I think of a patient, Jenny, who struggled to find a balance between love and hate on the court. She was first referred at thirteen because of her poor academic performance, the result of overwhelming anxiety when she was confronted with any kind of paper or exam. Early in treatment we had come to understand those problems as symptomatic reactions to the conflict between her parents and to their divorce when she was seven. Her very young mother, only seventeen at Jenny's birth, resented the curtailment of her own adolescence and the loss of independence built into taking care of Jenny and the brother born only eleven months after her.

Suffice it to say that Jenny's early years were filled with chaos and noise of the emotional and physical kind, complicated by her mother's favoring of her brother and by her over-indulgent father's attempts to downplay conflicts by buying things. But most formative for Jenny was her mother's continued acting out of her resentments: she neglected almost all parental and domestic chores, thrusting Jenny, remarkably conscientious and practical, into the caretaker's role, which she accepted while fearlessly persisting in pressing her defiant mother to pick up the slack. Frequent battles between mother and daughter became the norm, encounters that often escalated from verbal to physical on the part of the mother and bordered on abuse.

Jenny's mother would explode with rage if Jenny complained about the lack of food (her mother would rarely market, so Jenny did), the accumulated laundry and dishes (her mother refused to do either, so Jenny did both), and the pervasive disregard of the children that enabled her to spend long hours at the tennis courts indulging a passion that bordered on addiction. This had not stopped Jenny or her brother from becoming competent players, although in our first go-around together, tennis never came up except in terms of its centrality in her mother's neglect.

Several years after she married, Jenny called to resume treatment; she was frightened by her anger at, and frequent battles with her husband, battles that replicated the explosions between her mother and her. Picking up where she had left off, Jenny soon began to complain that she had mysteriously gotten the shakes during a weekend of tennis with her husband and some friends; she was bewildered. How come she could rise to great heights when competing with her mother or her brother but fell apart while playing with others, especially her husband?

Flashing to my own history where aggression had been punished or suppressed, I marveled at the arcane workings of the psyche and the differences between Jenny's experience and mine. Unlike me, Jenny could relish playing out her aggression on the court against the very person whose uncontrolled fury she had battled for years; winning for her could be a triumph that expressed her wish to "beat" and symbolically destroy her mother in return. Yet when it came to facing an unknown, Jenny unconsciously feared the damage she wished to do and could respond only with panic—a plight all too familiar to me.

Aggression and its fallout, I am convinced, was the dominant subtext of what was going on during the tennis finals with my best friend at camp, self-sabotage and all. It was a theme whose variations would flourish for much of my life—the consequences of growing up in a household where my father's conviction that reason is the baseline from which we should run our emotional lives reigned unchallenged, where the emotional distance (product of the reign of reason) ruled out the kind of engagement that would have allowed me to experience and survive forays of aggression, where I had to suppress and deny anger at all costs—all this began to surface during

Color War. By that time, winning was already too close to crushing or destroying another for me to tolerate or handle it.

I would, of course, have told my parents about the match but according to the code that made it impossible for me to think about competing aggressively, let alone to articulate my feelings of panic or hate, the conversation would have been limited to the facts, nostalgically punctuated by the singing of camp songs at the dinner table by my sister and me. To my expression of disappointment that I had lost the match even though my team had won, my father would have produced a comment expressing mild regret followed by his philosophical shrug and smiling query, did I have fun and had I done the best I could? It was his way of accepting our limitations and the way in which I believe he accepted his own.

It seems to me my father's profoundly simple guidelines served him well. His impulses and passions were so filtered through the organizing prism of reason and moral purpose that his behavior was the embodiment of his convictions. But I was clearly made of lesser stuff, and starting with the afternoon of the tennis finals, it seemed to me more and more that I fell short of the mark, sometimes in performance but always in my inability to accept disappointments with equanimity, or to comfort myself with the thought that I had done my best.

Today I know there was no way I could have allowed myself to win the match: the eruption of my overwhelmingly violent feelings persuaded me that I had violated some fundamental principles of the universe and filled me with guilt and shame. I could not allow a complete victory because I had to punish myself for the aggression embedded in the wish to win. At the time I was only aware of confusion, but now I perceive that what I did in salvaging the second set and losing the third was to strike a bargain, that is, to forge an unconscious compromise between the conflicted parts of myself. It was a compromise that became a template for many such outcomes in my tennis game and my life. Today I can appreciate and even admire its exquisite economy and fine-tuning: it allowed me partial gratification of my wish to win but deprived me of a full triumph in keeping with my guilt about violating the injunctions I had already internalized as my own.

There is no way I could ever have conveyed any of this to my father who would have been stunned to learn that the benevolent maxims he had presented to his children could convert to something so intensely complex. Of course, I could not have articulated it back then anyhow since awareness about myself and my game was confined to what could be accessed via reason, that is, my reflections and conclusions were severely limited by the tools at hand. Thus, unsettled as I was by the match, I soon supplanted my feelings with the somewhat uneasy rationalizations that tennis was only a game, and soon afterward, that I was a person who couldn't compete, not because I lacked the skills but as a reflection of temperament: once undone by nerves, I always would be undone by them.

That identification was reinforced several summers later when Elwood Cooke, a former champion and pro with whom I'd been taking lessons, suggested that I try out in a local tournament. Without any preparation, psychological or otherwise, beyond the validation that Cooke thought I was good enough, I was blown off the court in the first round, my humiliation compounded by the ease with which Cooke's assistant who also tried out, reached the semifinal rounds.

After that, my explanation about myself broadened from "unable to compete" to "intrinsically not competitive," a wildly erroneous rationalization that today fills me with poignant amusement about my naivete. But how often is one ever aware of such a defense as denial which is designed to protect one from the very fears and anxieties one cannot face?

In the best of all possible developmental worlds, tennis might have provided a pocket of safety for free play, but in mine, it became a playing field for my struggle to find a place where I could be myself without betraying my father and the internalized standards he represented. No small feat psychologically speaking and much of what my life has been about. Here I'm referring to the universal task of becoming one's own person, which for me meant separating and individuating from the father whose exemplary presence endowed me with a chronic sense of failure about ever being good enough. For all my education and actual achievements, reconciling those disparate parts of myself and their perceived undercurrents of incompetence in relation to authorities, those who "know," has been at the heart of my experiences on the couch.

But before that could begin, I first had to fall out of the kingdom of my father.

That opportunity emerged when I fell apart in college under the impact of exposure to new people and a world that contrasted markedly to the one in which I had grown up. As my initial excitement faded, I gradually became overwhelmed by my inability to tolerate or resolve discrepancies between that outside universe and my internal one—of expectations, prohibitions and ideals based (need I say it?) on my father as the rule and the norm. Before that, as a freshman at Radcliffe, a sense of excitement and accomplishment prevailed throughout most of that first year. Although I suffered torments when it came to writing (what was there of value that I could think or say), whatever anxieties I'd had about my ability to manage academically were somewhat assuaged with the first round of papers and exams. I'd also fallen in love with Cambridge with its old Victorian houses and gracious sense of time and space, and while there was some undercurrent that I would never feel at ease, I felt that I had definitely settled into life away from home.

Better yet, during that spring I met a charming non-lawyer graduate student working toward his Ph.D. Five or six years older than I, Jonathan was sophisticated, intellectually curious with a wry sense of humor about himself and life. On long walks and during meals in the Miró-decorated graduate-student cafeteria (amid the jokes I pretended to enjoy about the phallic symbols inspired by the murals), I mostly listened—to educated banter and esoteric talk between Jonathan and his friend Will, chiefly about the Renaissance while I remained surprised at Jonathan's sustained interest in me. If I continued to feel somewhat out of my league, at least I was on the way to growing up, or so I thought.

But not quite, at least when it came to sex. Our mutual attraction (sexual and otherwise) was strong and while I was certain that I loved Jonathan, I refused to go all the way. Close, but not the real thing. Then when he began to talk about marriage and suggested I transfer to the small college in another state where he would start to teach the next fall, his proposal became a loose string that began to unravel a tangled ball of yarn. For one thing, none of it seemed quite real. For another, as the end of the term approached, my period was a few days late. Convinced I was pregnant, I plunged into a well of panic and despair even though reason should have told me otherwise—after all, I hadn't actually had intercourse. But reason was gossamer against the weight of fantasy and near-hysterical fear.

Such a fantasy is not that uncommon and, in fact, is rooted in the magical primary process thinking that is the dominant mode of our earliest years. Consider the question the five-year-old girl asks her father after he tells her the facts of conception: "daddy, does the woman get to keep the penis after the man has deposited the sperm?" Or the words of Jane Hamilton's grown character Alice in *A Map of the World:* "Because I knew that my mother had had me in a hospital, and because, like all children I was not rational, I had the idea that the two events, the birth and the cancer were linked, and that I was responsible. I'm not sure I've ever really forgiven myself for her death…"

Many of us never fully outgrow these fantasies, and indeed they can often be a source of creativity in child or adult. But for me as an adolescent, mired in earlier conflicts when it came to matters of sex and sexuality, they contributed to my sense of shame and un-conscious guilt about loving a man other than my father, sexually or any other way. And in the pre-revolutionary nineteen-fifties, when Harvard men were not allowed upstairs in the Radcliffe dorms except once a semester when we had a formal tea, covert sexual explorations for some (like me) carried a charge of immorality and sin.

So for me, the wish or the coming-close felt the same as the deed, and in the absence of over-the-counter pregnancy tests or legalized abortion, I faced several weeks of agonizing uncertainty—never mind that Jonathan reassured me that we would find a way to deal with a pregnancy, or that having already asked me to marry him, he suggested that we could just move the timetable up.

That prospect actually made me feel worse: emotionally I was light years away from the differentiation or independence such a decision would entail. I couldn't imagine how I could chose to be in a relationship that would separate me from my past. How could I? I had arrived at college thinking my parents had an ideal marriage, nor could I even fathom how the several engaged girls in my dorm had been able to make the leap. Fortunately, reprieve came with my period just as I was about to take the pregnancy test Jonathan had arranged, and with the end of the term and enormous relief, I went home to a summer of tennis and hanging out, mostly sanguine about my successful year.

Not long after, I began to feel empowered. For the first time since puberty had struck at ten (way too young) and morphed me from being thin and the tallest girl in the class (which I loved) to someone one whose body I hated, that summer I had been able to stick to a diet and lose weight. Gone was the envy of my mother who seemed able to eat sandwiches and dessert or of the high school classmates who could put away ice cream sundaes dripping with chocolate sauce at lunch each day and stay thin; gone was the sense of deprivation that led me to have "just" a cookie or two before bedtime or "just" one doughnut after basketball practice on my way home (after all, I had just exercised the extra calories off). Even more astonishing, I began to feel completely in control—of my body and my desire for food.

I began my sophomore year confidently upbeat. (The odd sense of alienation I was starting to notice I attributed to my separation from Jonathan who was now at another college several hours away and whom I saw only on the occasional weekend—nothing more.) By late fall, I had shed some thirty-odd pounds (including the freshman fifteen I'd gained) and I hoped to lose at least fifteen more to give myself a cushion, to allow for a slip.

Underneath was a goad—my father's silent annoyance at my indulging in dessert when I was trying to lose weight, a familiar echo of his irritation at my aunt who was overweight all the years she lived with us, always causing him to shrug with disbelief that she lacked the necessary self-control. Just a few extra pounds, I kept reassuring myself as the scale kept sliding down (115, 110, then below), all the while believing myself thoroughly in control. By then I felt full after two or three mouthfuls and my desire for food seemed perfectly contained. It is the anorectic's paradox to feel so ultimately in control as she spirals out.

Anorexia has multiple components among which a denial of sexuality is key. It certainly played a role in my case, given my conflicts and guilt about sexual desires and my having come so close to acting on them. Perhaps even more important, it united me with my father who, not surprisingly, was about food as he was about everything else—in control. As I heard often enough growing up, when he was in his late thirties, he suffered an excruciating attack of gall stones and to avoid another, his doctor told him to stick to simple foods—baked, broiled, no sauces or fats. And so my father did, abandoning cold-turkey his young trencherman self, the one who relished eating and delighted in putting away abundant amounts, of a very thick outside cut of roast beef, veal schnitzel à la Holstein with two fried eggs on top, apple pie à la mode and sometimes seconds. This father was only hearsay by the time I was born. (An undated photograph: a solid, handsome man in his thirties with a full head of dark curly hair stands at ease, hands behind his back, a subdued but definite smile on his face. This was not the father I knew.)

The one I grew up with was bald and thin, at times to the point of emaciation. Of average height (5'9") and weight until his mid-thirties, he became quite thin and in later years slightly stooped, even frail, giving the impression of a simple, plainspoken man. Most of the time his expression was serious bordering on severe, for he did not have an easy sense of humor, let alone of the ridiculous or the sublime. However, when he relaxed (which required a before-dinner-drink after a long day's work), a warm and wonderful smile lit his face, softening its otherwise angular features and Lincolnesque lines so often touched by fatigue.

When he was struggling with a difficult opinion, his weight usually dropped even lower, as though he were being literally consumed by his work, prompting my mother to complain about how cadaverous he looked. To this he paid scant attention and I wonder (though I may be projecting here) whether he took some secret delight in maintaining his low weight. He certainly was compelled to check it: in the days when there were penny scales outside drugstores or on the subways, he could never pass one without stepping on it, this despite the fact that he had a doctor's balance scale at home (a birthday present from my mother one year), on which he weighed himself faithfully every morning and night, even more than that on weekends. It was this very same scale that was the source of horror for me one morning when I was in high school and discovered that I had topped my father's tell-tale morning mark of 139 pounds. For all the years that I have been on the thinner side of thin (most of my life), that memory still makes me cringe.

But cured I am not. Cured would mean I could occasionally eat a complete dessert instead of nibbling on someone else's or gain a pound or two with the knowledge that I could take it off. Instead, I try to bypass this lingering part of my neurosis by never getting on a scale, for once I see the numbers, I can become enslaved to every half-pound the scale might move—if up, the terror of gaining, if down, the excitement of a win that makes me want to go for more. Then I might start to weigh myself every day, then several times a day, to reassure myself that I am in control. So although I eat appropriate amounts of food and really love to eat, I'm definitely not cured.

Not surprisingly, my father's habits also ruled our household when it came to eating: he, so of course we, never ate food with sauces, Italian, French or any other kind. (Not even Chinese, to the amazement of Dr. Stevenson when early on I described our restricted exposures to food as more evidence of my father's pervasive impact. To this information, Dr. Stevenson had teasingly asked, "What Jewish child growing up in New York do you know who did not eat Chinese food on Sunday nights?" prompting me to quip back, *me*, delighted for once to know more about me than he.) The only exceptions to my father's regimen were the occasional scoop of ice cream for dessert, the piece of after-dinner chocolate to satisfy his sweet tooth, and the legendary blueberry muffins his clerks vied to provide (one even baking them himself) for mid-morning recess in Chambers.

Was it any wonder that my inability to control my eating differentiated me negatively from my father or that my success at dieting brought me back into the approving fold? So when I was able in college to adopt my father's restraint toward eating, I felt euphoric about my new-found control and the slim body it produced. But it was not long before my mood took an inexplicable downward turn. None of my courses held any interest for me even though I had selected them myself and a pall seemed to have descended on everything else. At some point I wondered vaguely whether what I was experiencing might be the traditional sophomore slump, although ever-conscientious, I continued my routines.

As the fall semester progressed, however, I began to be bored, filled with a malaise that seemed to apply to everyone and everything, even on the weekends when I visited Jonathan or he, me. The more he tried to reassure me about our future together, the worse I began to feel: instead of comfort and closeness, I experienced alienation and despair; overwhelmingly lost and tearful much of the time without knowing why, hoping for relief, I decided to stop seeing him.

Frequent phone calls home failed to make a dent in my fear, adding bewilderment as well: my parents were unable to fathom what had happened to the exuberant child they thought they knew (the one who charmed our dinner guests, who could make my father laugh when sitting on his lap, who learned with excitement and quick ease). But she, I was to discover, was a split-off external version of who I was, an extended illusion, a myth that had endured through my high school years which were actually a time of self-doubt, considerable misery and dislocation for me.

This type of crisis is not uncommon in later adolescence, the time when we consolidate the tasks of separation and individuation that begin at the moment of birth. The process never really stops but in adolescence it can be acute as we try to elaborate and confirm an identity apart from parental figures, to develop our own standards, to deal with the loss entailed in separation and to explore the sexual self—under the best of circumstances, a complicated series of inter-woven developmental tasks. For some it is primarily a phase, for others it can stir up earlier unresolved issues that may rupture in a crisis of identity and self. And that is what happened to me.

My successful negotiation of the first year of college had been only skin-deep. Just underneath lay my inability to differentiate from my family on almost any or every dimension, which included an incapac-ity to tolerate, much less explore, the unknown. While it saddens me to remember the constraints that kept me from throwing myself into what could otherwise have been an expansive time, and while I can still conjure up the bleak dark cloud that prevailed for several years afterward as I picked up the pieces and went on with the business of life, I have no doubt that falling apart was the best thing that could have happened to me. Naturally, that was not at all a perspective I could have at the time; instead I felt disorganized and overwhelmed, uprooted from the familiar order and constants of my life.

Whether or not being "crazy" is a developmental necessity of adolescence as Anna Freud has suggested, the diagnostic and man-agement questions in the face of symptoms are real. Should a par-ent ride out the crisis as a phase or intervene? And if intervene, in what way? Given the average adolescent's push toward indepen-dence, how does one get close enough to ascertain the "normality" or pathology of what is going on? Obviously, there are no universal answers in light of the "craziness" and different degrees of denial among people confronted with behaviors alien or unknown. For some adolescents, support from a teacher or coach may suffice; others may require someone more knowledgeable or trained such as a therapist, which fortunately was the case for me.

When my perplexed parents realized that none of the interventions at hand brought any clarity about what was happening to me (not even the prospect of a transfer to Barnard from Radcliffe, which I had proposed so I could again live at home), they arranged through a friend who was knowledgeable about such matters for me to have a consultation in Cambridge with Dr. Helene Deutsch. Among the many who had fled Europe just before World War II, as I would discover years later, she had become one of the doyennes of psychoanalysis here.

About the consultation I remember next to nothing except that, thin and out of control, I cried my way through—that, and Deutsch's formidable yet comforting presence. Yet whatever I spilled out was enough for me to feel that finally someone knew something about what was happening to me, and beyond that, that something could be done. Toward the end of our meeting, Deutsch calmly asserted that I needed help and that she would refer me to someone who could provide it, straightforward words that suffused me, in the midst of my agitation, with the prospect of relief.

To my surprise, I learned something more of that consultation only a few years before my mother died. By then, her usual vagueness had merged with the early stages of Alzheimer's, frustrating my hope for a more textured recollection. I'm not even sure how the subject came up but suspect I must have raised it since my mother was not forthcoming when it came to exploring the underside of things. Still, she did recount a part of the story I never knew.

Afterward, Deutsch had walked me to the anteroom where my mother was waiting and asked to see her alone, to fill her in, I assumed, and also to give her the promised referral for me. But Deutsch said much more: she told my mother that without intervention, I would kill myself—a part my mother had held back all those years. Not having been present, I can't be certain whether Deutsch said "could" or "would" or what she had in mind, yet I am sure that I wasn't suicidal in an active sense. Nor did I ever entertain suicidal thoughts. But I certainly didn't deny my distress in her office and it is indeed true that anorexics are capable of starving themselves to death. While anorexia had not yet entered the public awareness (which prompts me to acknowledge a rather perverse pride in being ahead of the times rather than a copycat), Deutsch undoubtedly recognized its lethal potential if left unchecked.

Occasionally I've fantasized a kind of collegial post-mortem with Deutsch in which I ask her whether her dire prediction had more to do with my mother than with me. Did she recognize that treatment was beyond my mother's ken and that anything less drastic than the threat of suicide would not produce the desired response? Had she sensed how naive my mother was when it came to matters of the mind, how limited and afraid she was of the unknown? Whatever Deutsch had in mind, she must have thought it necessary to emphasize that mine was not an ordinary diet that would right itself in due course as my parents undoubtedly hoped or thought.

My speculations about my mother's role in all this are reinforced by what occurred back in her hotel room after the consultation with Deutsch. (My mother had come to Cambridge alone while my father had remained behind to work—revealing, considering the severity of the situation I was in.) As we prepared to part, my mother to return to New York and I, weepily to my dorm, I tried to talk to her about what had been happening—my weight loss, my inability to stop crying, my dysphoria about school and my pregnancy scare along with my confounding disclaimer that I hadn't actually had sex, as well as the breakup with Jonathan whom I still loved. But after listening to what could only have been a confused outpouring of woes (how could I articulate what I didn't understand?), instead of giving me a reassuring hug, my mother blind-sided me with the pronouncement, "I'm not going to tell your father that you had sex with your boyfriend; it would kill him."

Stunned by her grotesque distortion of what I had tried so hard to convey, I didn't wonder until much later why my mother had focused on my perceived sexual misconduct rather than offer me some comfort in the face of my misery. Eventually, I would connect her behavior to the occasion several years earlier when she exposed my sister to the judicial wrath of my father on discovering that she had had sex with her boyfriend of several years. Did my mother really believe it would kill my father to know I might have had sex (or even come close) or was she the one to whom such knowledge was unbearable? Noticeably lacking (in retrospect only) was any softening touch on her part to help him get over his shock and cold rage.

In those days I certainly didn't know how someone could put her own feelings into another and be convinced that they originated there. Projection is a slippery and nasty defense, presumably compounded in this instance by some envy on the part of my mother of which she would have been unaware. (Other defenses are more detectible—forgetting someone's name as a way of killing him off when one is angry, or turning something into its opposite, like being compulsively neat when the real impulse is to mess.) So I'm not sure whose sense of dire sin was embedded in my mother's haunting comment, hers, my father's or both. But in the face of their rigid attitudes about sex, the punishing demands of my own too strict conscience did not start to quiet until I began therapy with Dr. R.

I liked him from the start. A comfortable, soft-spoken man, Dr. R immediately seemed a gentler, more benevolent version of my father. Like my father he was bald and wore bow ties, facilitating the positive transference that instantly took hold. But unlike my father, he encouraged me to talk about things that no one ever had before. So even though I felt awkward for the longest time (which situation I dealt with by bumming cigarettes from him as I sat across his desk*), I also began to feel that whatever had overtaken me could be remedied.

During the next several months, things slowly began to make a different kind of sense, and as the end of the academic year approached, Dr. R suggested that I consider deepening our work and undertake a psychoanalysis in the fall. Of course I knew next

---

*I really never smoked, except for a brief period in situations when I felt ill at ease and even then, I never inhaled. This was definitely an identification with my father who used to puff on unlit cigarettes which his unknowing new law clerks, to their chagrin, would often try to light. At some point as a child, I had exacted a promise from my father to smoke a cigarette on my twenty-first birthday; when the time came and we celebrated at an elegant restaurant in Boston, at my prompting toward the end of the meal, he did light one up. However, he was so awkward and uncomfortable that after his first puff, I suggested he put it out which he did to everyone's relief, including mine.

to nothing about what that meant: it sounded rather intimidating but also important and somehow made me feel worthy. So, with the approval of my parents (especially my father who footed the bill), I agreed, grateful to have found someone who seemed to offer a different way of thinking and give new meaning to who I was.

Which is how I found my way to psychoanalysis—the momentous *before* and *after* in my life. With it, the crisis receded, and the end of my childhood began to unfold in a more felicitous way. That's why I say that falling apart was the best thing that ever happened to me: first it created the opportunity, and then psychoanalysis provided the forum for me to recognize why things had taken the turn they had, and gradually I learned to confront, then even to embrace, the enormity of the invisible and unconscious forces in our lives.

Ultimately, psychoanalysis conferred the psychological freedom that gave me the blessed capacity to tolerate comparisons with my father and his ideals without automatically feeling diminished or small. It mostly put an end to my chronic sense of humiliation or shame both on and off the tennis court and became the prism through which I began to see myself and others more multi-dimensionally. And last, but surely not least, psychoanalysis is what imbued me with the passion and conviction about matters of mind that animate my life.

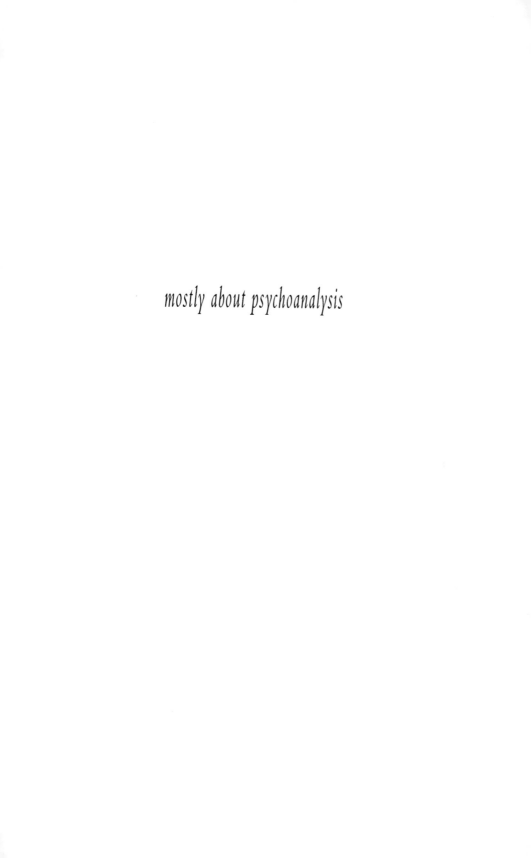

mostly about psychoanalysis

...a psychoanalysis is not a scientific investigation, but a therapeutic measure. Its essence is not to prove anything but merely to
alter something.

Freud, S: "A Phobia in a Five Year Old Boy"
(SE, Vol. X, p.104)

...during the progress of a psycho-analysis, it is not only the
patient who plucks up courage, but his disease as well; it grows
bold enough to speak more plainly than before. To drop the
metaphor, what happens is that the patient, who has hitherto
turned his eyes away in terror from his own pathological produc-
tions, begins to attend to them and obtains a clearer, more detailed
view of them.

Freud, S: "Some Characteristics of Obsessions"
(SE, Vol. X, p.223)

So what is psychoanalysis and how does it work? Yet again, I have vaulted ahead of my story by following the logic of psychic time and space, of theme and context, not unlike what happens in the therapeutic setting, where one jumps in and then wanders back and forth between the past and the present. The unconscious is timeless and if we can relax the bounds of reason, we can access a universe where odd connections are binding, where contradictions coexist, where a wish is the same as a deed, where absolutes of good and bad rule, where actual reality matters less than what our internal reality decrees.

It was this universe into which I landed during my adolescence, betrayed by my assumptions that reason and logic could explain all. "I believe in solving my own problems," I had self-righteously retorted when the girl next door in my dorm declared as we were getting acquainted that she had been in psychoanalysis throughout high school. The following year, no less antagonistic to anything psychological, I declined her invitation to join her at a series of seminars conducted by Anna Freud, lecturer-in-residence that term.* Scornful of what I didn't know, I had almost fully incorporated my father's version of the world.

---

*This is worth at least a footnote and has to do with a road not taken. After I had become a professional and realized what a golden opportunity I had missed, I rued the ignorance that had kept me from having first-hand contact with the daughter of Freud, a remarkable figure in her own right. But sometimes one can undo a regret. Quite a few years ago I noticed a newly published book, *The Harvard Lectures*, edited by Joseph Sandler, a long time colleague and collaborator of Anna Freud. Every lecture but her first had been transcribed almost verbatim and of course I immediately read the book straight through, admiring the simplicity and economy with which she had articulated some of the earliest aspects of development. I had indeed, missed out on something quite special. Still, discovering the transcribed lectures allowed me those many years later to share them with students in my own courses who, in turn, were delighted by Anna Freud in her own voice.

Since then, I have made the proverbial 180-degree turn, which actually, paradoxically, sometimes does me in professionally, at least on those occasions when, unable to put my own passion sufficiently on hold, I try too early on to persuade my therapy patients to undertake an analysis instead. Even though experience has taught me to trust that an analysis can and will unfold naturally from the work, I often still have to tame the beast of my passion and reign myself in. That is not, however, the same as my saying I think that psychoanalysis is the only means for people to develop a healthy sense of self, although I do believe that most people would benefit substantially from undertaking one. And I certainly wasn't thinking it was the way for me to go when, in mid-life, I began twice-a-week therapy with Dr. Stevenson.

Already a psychologist and experienced psychotherapist, I wanted to address a pattern of mistakes in my work—an off-the-mark interpretation, a failure to pick something up. Often they seemed to follow a kind of "undoing" of my good work, a dynamic similar (I realized with some amusement) to my losses at tennis from a notable lead. Then too, in supervision I'd become aware of my discomfort with the anger of some of my patients and the degree to which I was suppressing my own. But for all my recognition of the patterns operating or of the parallels between work and play, I couldn't figure out why—until what started as a pragmatic commitment to address professional matters turned into a fives-times-a-week transformative plumbing of the depths that would catapult me into training to become a psychoanalyst myself, or, in transferential terms, to be like my analyst/father when I grew up.

That reminds me of a question Dr. Stevenson asked me early

on about whether I had ever considered becoming a lawyer, as my sister did in mid-life, around the same time I began graduate school to get my Ph.D. His question took me by surprise: I presumed that the answer should have been obvious to him by then and without missing a beat I responded, "Are you kidding? Who'd want to compete with him? What would be the point?" Of course I had no idea how literal my thinking was on this matter, little realizing that I had been competing with my father almost all my life, the contest in which (in my mind) I always lost.

Some friends, on learning I was in analysis again, assumed that I was doing it for training as if perhaps otherwise I might be unbalanced, to which I've thought, "No, the first one was about survival; this is the real one and has to do with my father and me." Of course, an analysis is an analysis is an analysis, no matter what the ultimate goal. However, unlike the first generation of analysts who undertook an analysis primarily for the sake of becoming one, nowadays, there's no distinction between the personal and the professional although the latter is definitely a requisite for becoming one in any established training institute. If we have not made the journey ourselves, have not uncovered and wrestled with our own demons, how can we be able to help our patients learn to understand and cope with theirs?

But whether undertaken for personal or professional reasons, for me the fact remains that it is through analysis that alternative possibilities can be unlocked and ghosts like my father converted into ancestors who neither haunt or plague us. Not, I should add, that a psychoanalysis can leave one conflict-free or put anything into anyone that isn't already potentially there, but that it can still forces that wreak havoc or make one feel dead, can facilitate more generous compromises about what we might have or do, or free up parts of the self that have been constricted or out of reach.

At his literary best, Freud referred to the process of psychoanalysis as a journey, undertaken by two people (the analyst and analysand) to understand the unconscious workings of the mind of one. An apt metaphor, it is based on a model of the mind that pertains to the vast empire of the unconscious and its derivatives, and the interplay of unconscious forces (conflicts, fantasies, wishes, anxieties, inhibitions) that the analysand gradually exposes to the analyst through the medium of free association, dreams, enactments, and transference projections of significant figures from his or her past. These the analyst receives in the *here and now* of the treatment setting, offering interpretations, clarifications, occasional questions and a non-judgmental acceptance and containment—all of which facilitate taking a closer look at that which each analysand brings.

And more. Over the course of the journey, the analyst will uncover the defenses that have been established to conceal or deny the unconscious forces and fantasies that organize our lives. In the process of recognizing and confronting these very old longings and patterns of defense, the analysand comes to know himself and is able to work through such internal demons as fear of being trapped, suffocated, humiliated, sexually provoked or abandoned, to cite just a few. Finally he or she becomes able to find better solutions to the conflicts or fantasies that have variously haunted, destroyed or inhibited a lifetime of relationships or functioning at work.

Since I have no doubt that the gift of treatment has helped me to become my own person, I want to be clear about what kind of treatment I mean, especially since the very term psychoanalysis is sometimes interchangeably and erroneously applied to the wide-ranging varieties of therapies that have proliferated since Freud (psychodynamic and otherwise). The psychodynamic therapies include the Contemporary Freudian (with which I identify myself), as well as the Relational, Interpersonal, Kleinian and Object Relations, to mention a dizzying few. Non-psychodynamic therapies, such as Cognitive Behavioral, for one, encompass those that focus on structured ways to manage the self toward achieving a particular goal—for instance, enabling someone who is afraid of flying to get on a plane, someone who is terrified of crowds to leave the house, someone who is bulimic to stop binging and purging. Clearly, such therapy can be helpful but is not the kind I mean.

I would also include the current psychiatric medical model among the non-psychodynamic, relying now as it does almost exclusively on medication to relieve symptoms like anxiety or obsessive-compulsive mechanisms or to regulate mood as in the case of depression. While once upon a time in America, psychiatrists were the only professionals who could train as psychoanalysts,* most psychiatrists now follow the model where medication is the first, and often primary line of treatment; therapy, if conducted at all, usually occurs no more

---

*Another digression here: while in Europe both medical and non-medical professionals could train to become psychoanalysts, in America until the 1990's, only psychiatrists or medical professionals could train in the accredited institutes of the day, such as the New York Psychoanalytic or become members of the American Psychoanalytic Association. That is to say, licensed psychologists and clinical social workers had to find training outside the then classic institutes and many formed their own. Then, over twenty years ago, psychologists won a class action lawsuit that challenged this exclusivity and could train in the accredited institutes which nowadays usually have a preponderance of non-medical candidates, both social workers and psychologists, as well as M.D.s.

than once a week and addresses the alleviation of symptoms through medication and management.

(Here I'm not questioning the appropriate use of medication in conjunction with ongoing dynamic therapy although I do deplore today's near-epidemic use or overuse of drugs without attention to underlying causes or effort to effect significant change. Although some few psychiatrists today still undertake analytic training, relative to psychologists and social workers, they number very few.)

For all the conceptually ambitious potential of psychoanalysis, the actual work of finding links between what appears on the surface and what lies beneath often focuses on the concrete, sometimes even the mundane. My work with Mr. Phillips, a long-term patient, is a case in point: often his lateness for a particular session (the mundane) seemed to me to have been set in motion by his having felt deeply touched during a previous one.

Whenever I suggested as much, he dubbed my comments "shrink talk," nothing to do with him: his delayed arrival (fifteen minutes before the end of the session) was purely a function of the phone call that had kept him at the office (the denial and the defense). Little by little, however, as Mr. Phillips remembered the material from a session before, such as the one during which he had wept about the death of an uncle to whom he had been close as a child, he soon came to realize how guilty he had felt on recalling that he had not said goodbye before his uncle went out on the evening he was killed—for which behavior Mr. Phillips had been unconsciously punishing himself ever since.

That guilt was compounded by other painful memories that Mr. Phillips usually resisted exploring, claiming that he "knew" all that stuff about his past. What new things about himself could he possibly learn and what was the point? Since feeling deeply not only stirred Mr. Phillip's shame but also aroused his anger at both of us about his having exposed his vulnerable side to me and prompted him to miss more sessions afterward, I often despaired of getting past his defenses. On the other hand, the fact that he was able to feel some excitement or even passion (other than the anger or impatience) did fan his faint hope that he could change; and that hope was buttressed by the undeniable evidence that he was punishing himself by unconsciously identifying with his unaccomplished father through failure at work. (The punishment was complex since Mr. Phillip's admiration and idealization of his more successful uncle further diminished his father in his eyes, compounding his shame and guilt.)

It took quite a number of years before Mr. Phillips's defiant indifference could recede as he began to be able to tolerate the feelings of closeness our work stirred in him. With that progress, his pattern of lateness or missing sessions receded partially, though never totally. Ultimately however, his continuing need to disrupt the treatment (a major symptom in his personal relations and business life) trumped everything else, in our work manifesting itself through another seemingly mundane but destructive behavior—failure to pay.

The analysis of Lucy*, another patient, demonstrates a different kind of link between the therapeutic present and the past. For

---

*The matter of what patients call analysts and vice versa often needs to be exploited in a treatment. Lucy had been on a first name basis with the former therapist who referred her to me on moving away, and so Lucy

(footnote continued on p. 72)

several years, Lucy lay rigid on the couch, transported almost immediately back to the hospital bed of her childhood when chronic kidney infections had led to invasive surgeries and traumatic separations that made her feel abandoned and threatened by annihilating loss. Except for the hospital staff who necessarily performed the very tasks that sometimes caused her pain, no one was around to comfort or sustain Lucy: her mother rarely came to visit, claiming in response to Lucy's pleas that she was following hospital rules.

When Lucy grew up and learned that her mother's claim was a lie, she experienced a paralyzing rage which returned full-blown in the early states of her analysis, the hated couch playing a central role. First, Lucy rejected it: unable to tolerate the constraints of lying still in the treatment setting, she would often get up and restlessly pace the room, converting the passivity of immobility that had characterized her childhood experiences to the restless action of the adult. And later, as she dealt with both her anxiety and her rage in the transference (directed primarily toward her mother but toward a passive father as well), gradually Lucy became comfortable enough to use the couch as the facilitator it is for most patients—a magic carpet to the past.

Some might say, why not make the therapeutic situation easier for Lucy, why not have her use the chair instead of the couch? That question reminds me of the story a prospective patient told me about a previous consultation when she asked the therapist why she didn't have a couch. To which the latter responded, "You wouldn't turn your back on a friend or lie down in ordinary social interaction, so why would you do that here?" The answer is, that in reviving

---

automatically used my first name, as I did hers. With patients who address me more formally, I use the corresponding mode of address (Mr. Phillips). As treatment proceeds, patients often shift from the formal to the familiar—which of course is more grist for the mill.

the old memories and working them through, ultimately Lucy was able to yield old defenses and to regroup—not just on the couch, but in her life.

It surely was so for me, if not immediately. Soon after I began therapy with Dr. Stevenson and was clearly on my way to analysis (catapulted really), having already increased my sessions to four a week, he suggested that I might think about trying the couch. Presumably, this was a most natural progression for someone who had been analyzed before and had been a practicing therapist for years. Not for me.

My transition to the couch was anything but natural and took many months. At first, I was so determined to avoid it that I replied to Dr. Stevenson's initial suggestion by asking (the tone jesting, the question quite serious) whether it was possible to have an analysis without using the couch. Never mind that I had been analyzed before; for some reason I felt a sense of dread. Indeed, I tried out the couch alone in my office several times over the course of my ambivalent resistance, sometimes imagining Dr. Stevenson behind me, to see if I could bear to lie down. (In a journal I kept at the time, numerous outpourings record my struggles, many mixed with shame because I assumed that my having been analyzed before should have made it not the big deal it became.)

It didn't take long to realize that I didn't want to become (in the transference) the insignificant child of the distant father who was married to his work and could not really listen or pay attention to me: at this early stage of the analysis, I still hungered to see

Dr. Stevenson's face. What was harder to get at and would take longer to emerge: I also didn't want to become yet again the child who spent seven marginalizing and tantalizing years in my parents' bedroom, where, in the evocative words of psychoanalyst Phyllis Greenacre, I suffered the humiliating and near crushing ambiguity of feeling at once *excluded-in* and *included-out*. (More about that defining experience later on.)

To those who might think that for all my early analyses and subsequent clinical training and practice I should have been more in tune with some of these unconscious reservoirs of my mind, I say—it just doesn't work that way. After all, we live inside ourselves and it's not so easy to oscillate between observer and observed. And in my case the transference and regressive pull that a psychoanalysis can bring about were compounded by unfinished business left from my earlier analyses (actually two back-to-back treatments which, to all intents and purposes, I tend to conflate into one—the second, in New York, which I began only a year or so after my termination in Cambridge with Dr. R.)

Besides, a psychoanalysis is not a precise or scientific affair. How can it be, when the tools involve such subjective variables as decoding, empathizing and interpreting, where the analyst's task is to listen with evenly hovering attention while deciding whether to question or comment—and while also constantly monitoring and in fact using his or her own feelings *(countertransference)* as a guide? And then there are the differences in training and experience along the way and the variations in theory or personal style.

Still, as I would point out to critics who denigrate psychoanalysis as unmeasurable and therefore insubstantial, recent studies in attachment theory, in neurobiology mapping the interdependence between the physiological and the psychological or even post-analysis studies to determine the efficacy of treatment, confirm the merits of attending to unconscious mind and the emotional rewiring that can occur. Moreover, for all its subjective elements, reliable principles of theory and technique can be taught, to which the individual clinician adds the experience and intuition that make psychoanalysis the art that it is. (Put any two or three clinicians in a room and you will get a discussion, if not a debate, of the efficacy or theoretical rationale underlying some interpretation, intervention, or lack thereof.)

What most fully characterizes a psychoanalysis however, and distinguishes it from other therapies (even psychoanalytically informed psychotherapy, although the boundaries between the two are increasingly blurred), is the transference, not its existence, but its intensity—much of which is fostered by the greater frequency of sessions and the use of the couch. Together those tools help generate a return to the past by deepening the connection to the analyst and reviving old feelings or actions that are played out in the here and now.

Transference, of course, is not created by psychoanalysis. On the contrary, transference and its manifestations are ubiquitous, whether we have internalized ghosts, conflicts or identifications (the kindergarten child who absent-mindedly calls his teacher "mommy" or the man with a tyrannical father who rebels against authorities at work). It is the psychic way of the world. But it is transference, along with the resistance it stirs, that powers an analysis along, "the force that through the green fuse drives the flower," as Dylan Thomas so elegantly captured in his poem of the same title.

Here too, I should add that resistance, despite its pejorative sound, is not a bad thing but a corollary of the transference, the contemporary incarnation of the various maneuvers (defenses) a person has developed and brings into the treatment with him or her. Of course, sometimes the expression of resistance through the transference can threaten the viability of the treatment itself, as it did in the case of Mr. Phillips whom we met earlier and who, as the oldest child of holocaust survivors, bore the brunt of the fallout of his parents' trauma in the form of guilt.

Damaged by their incapacity to nurture him appropriately, he was particularly enraged that his mother's repertoire was confined to stuffing him with food and indiscriminately overreacting to everything; because she was unable to help him learn how to cope, he retreated to fantasy solutions he was never able to achieve. No less affected by her constant criticism of his passive father, Mr. Phillips unconsciously wanted to deny his mother the satisfaction of his success lest she have more ammunition for denigrating the father whom he loved, albeit ambivalently.

Mr. Phillips welcomed his father's quiet gentleness in contrast to the hysteria of his mother but was deeply ashamed of his father's heavy accent and failure to flourish, the latter a guilty by-product of his having abandoned his own mother to certain death in Europe when he escaped at her insistence. Ashamed of his shame, Mr. Phillips had to punish himself by failing, and, in the absence of a positive enough parental figure with whom to identify, he guiltily continued to project his failures on to his parents and their incapacity to provide him what he believed he had needed and missed.

By the time we began to work when he was thirty-five,

Mr. Phillips was full of self-loathing. Much of his self-defeating, self-destructive history was organized around his need to withdraw in the face of conflict or disappointment. The maladaptive omissions of his professional life (not paying bills, not showing up on time, being unprepared) had left him feeling isolated and marginalized but for the longest time, he fought recognizing the contribution of his unconscious aggression to his lack of success.

Locked into a code of revenge that had him trying to prove that I was not a good-enough analyst/mother, Mr. Phillips resisted with all his might acknowledging that I might have a positive impact on him. In the transference, he tried to reduce me to impotence, reminding me that he was "a failaholic, incapable of change." (The unconscious can be brutal when it comes to self-punishment or shame.) Nevertheless, nourished by moments of closeness between us and by my tenacity in holding on to some hope that he could benefit from our work, Mr. Phillips continued to come and wrestle with the ancient sources of his misery (what Freud meant by working through).

A major turning point came for Mr. Phillips when he could recognize and acknowledge that he did not want to give me (his mother in the transference) the satisfaction of his getting better, even at the cost of sacrificing his gains. No way either of us could have weathered his need to defeat me, to prove anew by his failure to succeed in treatment with me how destructive the impact of his mother had been—were it not for our repeated cycles of undoing and repair (transference and resistance).

The example of Mr. Phillips also underscores the importance of the greater frequency of sessions which creates the frame that provides the necessary soil for interpretation and insight to take root and grow. The consistency of the setting, including the analyst as a neutral presence who neither criticizes nor judges in the here and now of the transference, allows us to reconcile conflicts without having to flee or fail. With the analyst's sustained tolerance and his or her interpretation of transference patterns and the resistance to uncovering them, the unconscious becomes conscious and enables us to cope in different and presumably in better ways. And thus, not by affecting the cognitive known, but by facilitating access to the emotional unknown, can an analysis be a vehicle of change.

Soon after my first session with Dr. Stevenson, I was catapulted into a domain of longing and anxiety; the time between sessions seemed endless, their number never enough. Irrational it was in the light of day, but near unbearable as I went through it—so much for intellectually understanding what transference is about!

My reaction to Dr. Stevenson actually was a major unconscious factor in my choosing him. Yes, my supervisor Dr. Edwards had cited Dr. Stevenson as "the best," but that had been in response to my having asked for a referral for my sister, to reassure me that she would be in good hands. (If Dr. Edwards had thought the referral was for me, he never would have used the superlative, knowing through our work how burdened I was by the omnipresence of my father and how fraught "the best" would have been. Indeed, those were chief among the reasons we agreed that I should undertake some therapy.) But my sister concluded she would prefer to work with a woman (unthinkable to me) and when I began to think about finding someone for myself a few months later, "the best" immediately came to mind. I did consult with several other people as Dr. Edwards suggested, but once I met and liked Dr. Stevenson, my transference fate was sealed. In the language of the trade, my reaction was "over-determined" from the start.*

That pull was further exacerbated because Dr. Stevenson seemed hard to get: toward the end of our consultation which occurred just before the August break, I asked about continuing in the fall, to which he said he wasn't certain he would have time and suggested I call after the summer's break. Primed as I already was to feel I could never measure up to "the best," his uncertainty about his availability tapped into the yearning and anxiety of the child who could never belong. Plain and simple, I was hooked: Dr. Stevenson and the analysis took over my existence in matters large and small.

Even so, when Dr. Stevenson would remark that the intensity of my reactions to him as "the best" was predominantly transference, for the longest time I could not really believe him; for at least the first half of the analysis I was in a state of heightened vulnerability and intense moods, consumed with thoughts about him. It felt like the real thing, an aspect of the process formally referred to

---

*Yet another illustration of the power of transference: soon after we began, I mentioned to Dr. Stevenson that it was originally my sister for whom Dr. Edwards had given me his name but that after consultations (including with him), she decided she preferred to work with a woman. I, however, convinced that I had found "the best" (therapist/father), felt very guilty—as if I had won out over her. So much for the facts in the face of unconscious mind, especially when it comes to sibling rivalry.

in the profession as regression in the service of the ego, that is, in the service of growing up.

It's supposed to happen that way—but not so abruptly. For all that I continued to live my life with family and work, my dramatic immersion in the transference was quite unlike Freud's vision of a gentle departure on the journey agreed upon between analyst and analysand that only gradually gathers momentum and speed. To one complaint about the intensity that gripped me, Dr. Stevenson commented that "it's supposed to happen that way," to another, that perhaps I had some "unfinished business" left from my previous analyses; more often I thought wryly that I had fallen down Alice's rabbit hole or been caught up in a wrinkle in time.

From that perspective (of my own experience), when one of my patients is at the beginning of that long process with me, I often wonder who in his or her right mind would undertake such an arduous journey with no guarantees. It's really a huge leap for some, requiring the courage to trust that he or she will not be treated in the old familiar ways; some people are so fragile that they lack even the capacity for hope, in which case it is the task of the analyst to hold on to it for them. While the threat of being trapped or humiliated by being known might make some analysands want to flee, for me, the fact that there was a person whose very explicit role was to pay me the attention I so sorely lacked growing up, a person of whose work I was the object, made me want to stay in treatment forever, for the longest time, never knowing how long would be long enough. (It would be about halfway through a very long analysis before I could acknowledge that it, at some point, could and should end, and even longer before I began to think that I was ready. That time however, did come about.)

Still, love and longing are not the only things we transfer to the analyst. It can be hate, fear, anxiety or, all too often, the inability to fully love, whatever lies underneath the conflicts that bring us to analysis in the first place. Which brings into focus what Freud meant when he stressed the importance of the analyst's anonymity and neutrality. What he had in mind was to allow the largest possible space for a neutral screen on which the transference could emerge, neutral because, once we know the analyst (as a friend or a teacher) or know details about the analyst's personal life, the harder it is to sort out our fantasies and projections from the real, to distinguish transference reactions from those stirred by behavior of the actual person.

This is not to say that the patient does not develop a fairly accurate sense of who the analyst is or what he or she believes; indeed analysts today recognize the impossibility of preserving absolute neutrality since our attire, our office, and certainly our words or the absence of them are revealing. But it is quite different to have such knowledge evolve from the shared experience of treatment than from self-disclosures on the analyst's part. (I once overheard a woman euphorically praising her "shrink" to her lunch companion as she went on to describe her fantasy come true: she had invited him to her wedding and he had come. Eavesdropping shamelessly, and seriously frustrated that I could not set her straight, I discovered that he had divulged so much personal material to her that they sounded as if they were friends who met once a week, not analyst and analysand.)

The feelings of closeness that develop are certainly real and do grow over the long haul of the process. Recently, Dr. Z, a patient who had been in treatment with me for many years, began to talk about going it on her own, about undertaking the separation or process of ending which we analysts call *termination*. She had started the session by recounting a dream in which she had enrolled in a course but hadn't gone to any of the classes or taken any of the tests; she was worried that she might fail. None of it made sense to her since she had already graduated from college and professional school: what was she doing taking a course?

One of her associations had to do with the early days of her treatment when she was very angry about having to "sign up" for treatment, something anathema to her that she undertook only because she was in such pain and alienated from everyone and everything in her world. Recently, for work-related reasons entirely beyond her control, she had had to miss quite a number of sessions, for which, according to our arrangement, she was financially responsible (the course she's paid for and misses).* Dr. Z mused that she had been thinking for some time that perhaps she didn't need "the class" any more, and then she reflected loosely on what our work had meant for her.

Two things I don't like about analysis are the money or the time commitment. It used to be so scary but it's not any more. Now it.

---

*Once one has determined the frequency and the hours, it is customary to charge for missed sessions—no matter how much warning one might have—although with sufficient notice, most analysts do try to schedule a make-up. Since many patients often miss sessions due to some form of resistance, it is important to stay with the frame and to understand what is going on; while some do miss because of things that are out of their control, to distinguish between one type of missing and another unduly complicates things—not to mention that the fee is a source of income for the analyst and the hour is "reserved" for the analysand, no matter what—an essential aspect of the analyst's availability.

feels like a security blanket...will I need it forever? if I stop, will I go back to stewing alone? Who will I complain to if I don't have you?

I tell you this stuff that used to burn a hole in my brain. Now sometimes I tell you just to get rid of it...

When I was my kids' age, I never wanted to hang out with my parents...maybe it has gotten too comfortable here...or (teasingly)... maybe it was just my change of jobs that helped me...

The issues that brought me here are gone...I don't feel hopeless about my life...I don't feel terrified and angry...I feel good about my family...and there are no sharks outside waiting to attack...

She was silent for a few minutes so I asked her what she was thinking.

All of a sudden, my thoughts went blank. I have a tremendous problem with being ignored. I don't think I could have gotten much out of this if you had just pursued your agenda...you have had an impact on me but first I had to have an impact on you. I don't think I could have gotten much out of this—if you had been as rigid as I thought you were when we began. That was crucial...

Indeed, I had been rigid back when we began, which co-incided with the start of my analytic training at a time when I was quite locked into the one-dimensional model of analysis from my first experiences with it. However, early on in her treatment, Dr. Z was also projecting her parents' cruel indifference and rigidity into me. The truth was some place in-between as I had acknowledged to her at some point. Then she continued:

...A lot of the experience of my life has had to do with inflexibility on the part of others in relation to me. I would really like to think that I have had some effect on the way you think about what you do ...your acceptance has been enormous for me and that's not the same as unconditional regard...you didn't seem to hold anything against me—not when I attacked or hated you. I feel that you are absolutely reliably here. Can I get along without that? You know me better than anyone else...other people in my life see me through their own eyes and needs and there's too much distortion...

We were nearing the end of the session and after a long pause Dr. Z said,

...I'm going to miss you. That makes me feel sad...I feel like I'm going to cry.

To which I thought, I too was feeling a sense of impending loss and close to tears myself: I would miss Dr. Z, and as the time of actual termination came closer, I would acknowledge that to her as well.

As the example of Dr. Z suggests, patients aren't the only ones with feelings or transferences, and that brings me to *countertransference*, the analyst's contribution to the process, a significant, if less noted part of it, at least until relatively recently in the history of psychoanalysis. Indeed, Dr. Z provides a rather dramatic instance of what I mean: at the beginning of her treatment, she would often accuse me of lying about whether I had any feelings of anger toward her, convinced that I was suppressing my wish to attack her as members of her family often did. And as she frequently did to me in the first few years. She was right about my having feelings, but they were not her family's malevolent ones: back in the days when she was apt to explode with rage or tears at anything I did or didn't say or do, my feelings were definitely closer to dread. Indeed, I spent considerable time in supervision struggling with my dread of her anger, confused about the absence of my own, so much so, that one supervisor hit a bulls-eye when he remarked by way of encouraging me, that when I felt more comfortable with my own aggression, I would do much better with that of Dr. Z. Which indeed turned out to be the case.

It wasn't only Dr. Z's anger that intimidated me. I also struggled with my fears that I would fail her or that she would leave the treatment in view of what felt like my helplessness in the face of her emotional storms and my corresponding inadequacy to be effective with her. In those days, I little understood the importance of my just being there as a container or more important, the treatment's being able to survive her attacks.

Under the aegis of the classical model of analysis, Dr. Z would undoubtedly have been considered unanalyzable, but fortunately her treatment coincided with the revolution in the field that evolved not only to include a broader range of patients but also to encompass a broader definition of the analyst's participation. This is in keeping with contemporary recognition that the patient is not the only one affected by what is going on and it is often important to acknowledge as much to him or to her. Dr. Z was one who needed that kind of engagement and for the first few years, some acknowledgment of her reality, whether a response to her comment about the weather or a thank you when she complimented me about my clothes. (And once, when her drab manner of dress seemed to have significantly improved, even a compliment from me to her.)

The older model, where the inscrutable analyst only listened and after long silence dispensed wisdom from an Olympian throne behind the couch while the analysand accepted interpretations with appropriate awe or was said to be in a state of resistance until he or she did, would not have worked for Dr. Z. But whatever its limitations, even that more authoritarian process definitely opened up windows for me, especially as an adolescent in crisis who had no inkling that the analyst was anything other than the authority who knew. This belief was reinforced by the fact that the analyst almost never would ask, let alone answer questions, whether for information or clarification, as if he or she could divine all solely through free association and dreams.

It was in that era that unresolved feelings in the analyst about the patient were considered neurotic, something of which he should be cured, if necessary by resuming his or her own analysis until the difficulty was worked through. For Freud (who did not necessarily practice as he preached), the pitfalls and dangers of countertransference were a prime reason for the analyst to have had a good analysis of his own. Yet even that doesn't fully protect us, which is why so many of us meet regularly, in supervision or among ourselves, to talk about our work.

Today, most analysts acknowledge that countertransference is important to the process and grist for the analytic mill. Despite considerable difference of opinion about just how much to focus on the analyst's role and the relational or *intersubjective* component, there is general agreement that the analyst is part of a dyad (a pair) to which each contributes and in which both sometimes unconsciously act out together. (Among a plethora of examples, one such *enactment* might involve a patient who is delinquent about paying and an analyst who has trouble dealing with the subject of fees and avoids it, letting the debt pile up.)

I once supervised a fairly experienced candidate whose own difficulties around self-esteem and money got in the way of her confronting a patient who was several months behind in paying for his sessions. Although she was herself in analysis (the best place to explore the roots of the matter), it took much encouragement from me for her finally to screw up her courage to raise the issue. Her patient's initial response was anger but that was soon followed by relief, first that they were confronting their mutual omissions (he to pay and she to ask), and then, that he could cease withdrawing out of anger and guilt mixed with fear that she would retaliate by withholding her affection and concern. Acknowledging and exploring their joint enactment of their respective omissions in the safety of the analytic space galvanized the treatment and exposed an important dynamic: the patient had been repeating (literally and symbolically) what his sadistic father had done to him.

Of course, sometimes the proverbial cigar is just a cigar. That turned out to be the case on the singular occasion when Dr. Stevenson kept me ten minutes beyond the usual fifty, as I discovered only after I'd left and was halfway down the block. While one might imagine that I would have felt gratified or favored by getting extra time, just the opposite occurred: I felt acute panic, a fear that he liked me better (a fantasy) and that I had seduced him to break the rules. But after several minutes, much to my relief, I remembered that he had recently changed our schedule and realized that he'd simply ended the session at what would have been the original time. When I brought up my reactions in the following hour (which I never would have done in the very different days of my earlier treatment), Dr. Stevenson confirmed with a laugh that confusion had been the culprit; he too had noticed the mistake just after I left.

When I think back to my earlier analyses, I see that I was well-suited to the austere authoritarian model that prevailed back then. For instance, there was the way I handled the transition from sitting-up therapy to the lying-down psychoanalysis Dr. R recommended six months after we began. Constricted as I was and also intimidated by wanting to measure up to the more "grownup" process he thought appropriate for me, I found it painfully difficult to free-associate and for months I lay rigidly, mostly silent on the couch (as if rigor mortis had set in). So much so that after several months, Dr. R suggested that I sit back up: perhaps the time for an analysis was not right. His suggestion shocked me into action even though I knew he intended it in a non-critical way: dutiful daughter that I was, I immediately began to talk—to do the best I could, at least enough to get the process going along.

But I don't think I ever achieved a sense of freedom about saying what came to mind, not with Dr. R during my college years or with Dr. L, his successor, about a year later. That would only come about with Dr. Stevenson when the issues around and about the authorities in my life erupted in full force and I grew into the self who began to know and to say what was on my mind.

Without doubt, the matter of an analyst's authority and interaction with any particular analysand can be complex. Since giving advice is generally not the role of the analyst, it's a tricky business for the process when an analysand gets involved with something or someone representative of a repetition from the past that he or she cannot control. For this reason, in Freud's time and well into the fifties in this country, prospective analysands usually had to promise not to make any major life changes (a move, a marriage, even a new job), lest a dynamic that should have been reserved for exploration in session and worked through, be acted out in life.

Which is what happened with me and Dr. R who took that orthodox position about three years into the analysis: the issue was my relationship with a man who was a contemporary version of my father in terms of the emotional distance I could never close up with him. I was smitten at once with the interest of someone as handsome and charming as Peter, especially since he had already dated several of the more dauntingly sophisticated girls in my dorm. Although he was in law school, his passion for travel and writing convinced me that he would not be married to his work although he had, however, made it clear from the beginning that he couldn't or wouldn't make an emotional commitment, to me or to anyone else.

Peter's eventual acknowledgment that he was dating another woman at the same time as he was seeing me added to an already seductive mix, as did even more, his telling me that even though he wasn't sure he loved her, he'd probably marry her at some point. Matter over mind, I thought. What could be more compelling than a challenge to win out over her? So, enchanted by the familiar package of an attractive man who put other things and people before me, I kept hanging around—until Dr. R and I identified the pattern, which had little to do with my boyfriend and just about everything to do with my father and me.

Armed with the knowledge that ending the relationship was the best thing I could do for myself, with the encouragement of Dr. R, I did so. Or, more accurately, I tried. But back on campus in the fall after a summer interlude when Peter and I stayed in touch by writing to one another (what harm could there be in exotic letters from Spain where he had gone to immerse himself in the bullfights à la Hemingway, or in others that followed from San Francisco where he had gone as a summer associate with a prestigious law firm?), I lapsed and began going out with him again, thinking I could remain in control—of my feelings, that is.

But I soon found myself in session complaining about the yearning and sense of being out of control that had set in again. Whereupon, after a rather long silence, Dr. R sighed and firmly said that if I wanted to continue the analysis, I'd have to stop seeing the distant young lawyer-to-be: the place to work through my conflicts was in session, not outside. I was stunned but of course I complied with the edict from the man who in the transference had taken my father's place. Fortunately Dr. R's intervention (and attunement to the difficulties of breaking old patterns) pushed me off the perch on which I was stuck. While I now know how much anger I suppressed in typical fashion in response to his edict, I still have no doubt that my work with Dr. R did begin to lead me out of the binds of my past.

But for all that he and I accomplished, my advance into a present that was neither a disguised version of that past or a backlash would require considerably more work—which is why and how, back in New York some eighteen months later following another failed love affair, I found myself in the office of Dr. L. The precipitant was yet one more replay of my attraction to distant, ultimately unavailable men, this go-around, a handsome, dark, slight, cellist/lawyer I met over dinner at the home of friends of my parents who had thought we might hit it off, which we did.

The initial spark was fueled when John amicably agreed to my suggestion that we play duets (my piano to his cello), but as our duetting and mutual attraction grew he warned me, as had Peter before him, that he was not about to commit to anyone just then. He had just extricated himself from a ten-year relationship and was in analysis to understand his own tendencies to get involved with inappropriate partners.

"Inappropriate" couldn't apply to me, I thought, immediately sucked as I was into the orbit of his uncertainty (read distance) and determined that love would win out. For all that, I always felt on edge, uncertain of my place. And six months into our dating, John presented me with a beautiful pair of earrings that he dubbed "either an engagement present or a consolation gift" which, a week later he pronounced to be the latter as he broke up with me. (Notice that I yielded all the power to him.) The bad news was that I was devastated by my failure to get him to fall in love with me; the good news was that I recognized the pattern and called Dr. R for a referral in New York.

The route to one's analyst can be a circuitous affair. Dr. R suggested I call Dr. Green who saw me for a one time consultation and sent me on to Dr. James who saw me for a series of six or seven, the better to assess my analyzability and find someone who would have the necessary hours at fees I could afford. (Like the allemande right of a square dance, that's the way it was done in those days.) From the first, I didn't like Dr. James: bird-like, she sat perched in a huge armchair on the far side of the room and utterly demoralized me with a tactless summary of the results of the battery of psychological tests she had recommended: "You're very smart but emotionally very immature," (the latter clause the only part that resonated of course). Typical of my ready intimidation by authority in those days, I never considered that my feelings about Dr. James might warrant my seeking out another consultant, nor did it occur to me that they might affect my attitude about the person to whom she might refer me. Hence I didn't think to question her recommendation of Dr. L whom I called as soon as Dr. James gave me her name.

It was early in July and we agreed to meet, to look one another over as it were. There in a small office, not in the room with the couch, Dr. L sat behind her desk and I on the other side, describing what had brought me there.* Then we worked out the fee, the frequency (five times a week), the specific hours, and at the end of fifty minutes we shook hands and said goodbye. In September, I arrived for our first session at a different location and following a

---

*A number of years later but before my analytic training, I saw Dr. L briefly for supervision and discovered that I had been her first post-training analysand (hence the affordable fee). This also explained our meeting in the small office that in retrospect, was a transitional space for her. None of this would, or should I have known at that time.

nod from Dr. L, walked toward the couch, lay down, and the analysis began. The routine never varied after that.

"Please come in," the disembodied European-accented tones would echo into the waiting room and I would make my way to the adjoining office. There Dr. L would be standing next to her chair behind the couch on the far side of the room, as if she had not moved from the previous session, a fantasy, reinforced by the fact that the last patient would have exited unseen into a hall away from the waiting room. With her hand resting on her hip, she would simultaneously smile and nod as I made my way to the couch, the site of my predictable five- or ten-minute struggle to start to talk. Then, exactly twenty-five minutes into the session, or so it seemed, Dr. L would make some comment or interpretation that seemed to validate my words, and thus reassured, I could relax the undercurrent of anxiety that what was inside my head was nonsense or that I was not as smart or as serious as she. That was unanalyzed transference too.

Not once in our four years together did I think to mention the feeling of dread with which I began each session, born of my apprehension that my free associations were babble (the naive and insignificant child in the parental bedroom); nor did I ever really imagine that Dr. L could be off the mark or that I might disagree with her. In other words, I ignored my discomfort for the most part and suppressed whatever thoughts or feelings might have helped me get to the bottom of the role of the authorities in my life. As for lying on the couch: we also never discussed my experience there one way or another, and we certainly did not explore my anxiety about her power to crush me with the authority of her opinion—more transference to her as my father, of course.

But here, I must modulate the negative impression I'm conveying about my experience with Dr. L. At the time it was anything but, so it seems worth mentioning that the negative shift occurred quite a few years post-termination, in the context, I now believe, of my feeling abandoned by her when I gave birth. Before that and during the analysis, I was very much attached to her and while the longing was at once more diffuse and more contained than what I was to suffer later with Dr. Stevenson, our separations were also difficult for me. I would even search her out, constantly hoping to look over my shoulder and see her at the theater or bump into her on the street.

That fantasy was never realized during the analysis but a few months after termination it was: on a beautiful Sunday morning in the fall, my husband and I were taking a stroll in Central Park with our infant daughter in her carriage and Dr. L appeared from the opposite direction, arm in arm with a man, presumably her husband (about whom, interestingly, I'd never wondered). We all stopped and of course I was excited to show our daughter off. Although I had called Dr. L from the hospital after giving birth and been surprised and deeply touched that she had sent flowers, I had never thought to take the baby to 'meet' her as so many of my patients in this different day have done. So, despite Dr. L's protestations that I might wake the baby if I turned her from her stomach to her back, I happily did so, thrilled at the fantasy-come-true. (Afterward, ever greedy and as if showing off my daughter hadn't been enough, I turned to my husband and reproached him for not having shaved that morning, thus failing to look his handsome best!)

It is really only in the light of hindsight that I discovered how much of Dr. L's silence was sterile and intimidating, how on the defensive I felt and alone. Not that Dr. Stevenson hasn't been plenty silent as well or that I haven't had to battle anxiety in his office, particularly when it came to talking about my work and the agony of feeling so inadequate and exposed. That's unavoidable, essential to the process so that transference and fantasies can emerge. The difference is that with Dr. Stevenson, it was out in the open: for example, not only did I complain early on about feeling insignificant, but also he seemed attuned from the start to the ridiculous gap between my accomplished self and my fragile self-esteem.

Perhaps a journal entry from an early stage of my analysis with Dr. Stevenson will capture some of what I mean:

> *I think the difference between the first two analyses and this one is that I feel how crazy or childish/like I can be. It doesn't frighten me and it seems as if that's the way it's supposed to be...with Drs. R and L, I think I was always trying to prove how grown up I could get to be, but now it feels that I can grow up only if I can be a child. Time is out-of-joint or in-joint, but for sure, not in a straight line...now I keep dropping into pockets of intense feeling and mood with much unevenness. It's not bad, just different...*

For all that we accomplished in my early treatments, I still marvel at how much remained untouched, most notably the role of conflict and aggression in my life or anyone else's. But I remind myself that analysis back then simply did not deal with the underlying issues of self-esteem that derive from the earliest (pre-oedipal) formative years. (It is hardly coincidental that the fragility of self-esteem co-existed with my inhibitions about aggression.) To be fair, there will always be some aspect of the unconscious that does not get fully explored in any analysis, but the failure of my first treatments to address the roles of aggression and conflict seems not at all a minor thing to me. Yet each was terminated upon mutual agreement that I was "ready."

The time came about with Dr. R when, after staying on in Cambridge for a year beyond my graduation to continue analysis and to apprentice as a teacher at the Shady Hill School (which I loved and which, far more than college, opened up the possibilities of learning for me). However, I was unable to find a job there as I had hoped, but did find one in New York instead. So I reluctantly accepted Dr. R's pronouncement that I was a "mature young woman" ready to terminate although in my secret heart of hearts I felt he had let me go. (I did, however, cherish his parting remark that analysts become attached as well. Who would have thought—who would have allowed oneself to think then—that an analyst had any feelings at all?)

My experience around termination with Dr. L was more complex. Sometime in the fall of our fourth year together, by which time I had been married for about a year, I mentioned that I was thinking about becoming pregnant. Since my plan was to stop working after giving birth, I would no longer have money to continue the analysis and would have to stop. But instead of addressing that, Dr. L immediately focused on my thoughts and feelings about becoming pregnant, while my anxieties or ambivalence about ending analysis remained mostly unexplored. We never looked at what termination meant to me beyond its obvious connection to my taking a major life step: becoming pregnant was the happy analytic ending for those days.

Nowadays, by contrast, most analysts recognize the enormous vulnerability and potential for growth that maternity can bring and see the experience as a time for accomplishing a great deal of psychic work. Who better than an analyst to understand the depths and complexities of such a life-enhancing and -transforming event? Who better to provide the support a young mother (or father) might need?

But that was not where psychoanalysis was when I terminated with Dr. L at the August break six weeks before our daughter Elizabeth was born. Although I felt somewhat apprehensive, I believed that I had completed the crucial task of separating from my father, that I could function as a woman without being trapped or crushed as I perceived my mother to have been, and that I had acquired some significant tools, especially considering the naive adolescent I had been. Content with the work Dr. L and I had done, I remained unaware until much later that I had indeed felt abandoned by her, as though I had had to sacrifice what mothering she could have provided me when I became a mother myself. Later still, when my analytic training introduced me to the concept of the analyst's countertransference, I couldn't help wondering more about the role of Dr. L's own childlessness in her 'abandonment' of me.*

In the contemporary light of hindsight and the works of Klein, Winnicott, and others who have become so integral to understanding the psychic world, what I now know is that Dr. L's insistence

---

*How did I know Dr. L was childless? Quite a number of years after termination when I was doing therapeutic tutoring, I had asked Dr. L whether she would supervise me and we worked together for about a year (considerably pre-analytic training). It was then that I learned that she had emigrated to this country as a result of World War II, that she took care of her elderly mother and that although married, she had not had children of her own.

on my wish for a baby (which wasn't unconscious at all although some of my conflicts about having one were) shut out the significant domains of deprivation, envy and their consequences. Left as I was for more than two decades with pockets of unconscious turmoil in those areas, for all I had learned, I could not decipher the clues that kept getting in my way on the tennis court, especially since I considered myself to have been well-enough analyzed to have acquired the requisite tools to help me figure things out. Sometimes I could and I did, but for the most part I lived an uneasy truce with them, little realizing that significant pieces of the puzzle had been left unexamined and untouched.

Little realizing too, by the time I entered training after starting treatment with Dr. Stevenson some two decades later, that some of the conceptualizing ground rules about analyst and analysand might have changed, and with them, the experience of treatment itself. In addition to the analyst's primary role of interpreting and helping the analysand construct a narrative of his or her life, the analyst was now a good-enough parental object (transferentially speaking), even a new object, also a container for the feelings and anxieties that the analysis stirred in the analysand. Nor could I have imagined that the particulars of the relationship would depend to some extent on unique dynamics that Boesky, a superb clinician, has written, "could never occur in any other analytic pair." Even the very idea that each analytic dyad might have its own singular chemistry contrasted with the old implied principle that a good-enough analysis with the same outcome would ensue with any analytic pair, as if all well-trained analysts and their analysands were readily interchangeable parts.

This new conception of the analytic pair quite challenged my fixed idea, rooted in the power of my relationship with my father, of the analyst as *the one who knew* and kept the analysand in check; it also dovetailed with my view of myself as someone who could never know enough. I certainly had no idea when I began with Dr. Stevenson that my model would grow to incorporate the creation of a space within which analyst and analysand could accomplish their work in a fluid variety of ways. And that discovery would also lead to my recognition that it would not be mastering the rules of theory and technique that would turn me into a good-enough analyst (my index for measuring up to those authorities who had gone before me) but about finding my way with each particular analysand, using the structure of the treatment and contemporary theory as I would come to understood it in more flexible and at times expansive ways—not instead of transference and resistance—but in conjunction with them.

At the start of the analysis with Dr. Stevenson, locked in as I was to the ancient issues of admiration and awe, I certainly could not have imagined that I would end up challenging him to a match on the tennis court with a sense of comfort and delight, not literally of course, but with the vocabulary of play that had evolved through our work in the safe arena of the analytic space. None of which could have unfolded without the essentials of the analytic process, the frequency with which we met, the continuity, and the trust that grew from that.

So here's what I have in mind when I refer to psychoanalysis: a bare-bones minimum of three sessions per week, more optimally four, and ideally five—that's the frame. On a micro-level, I should add that the frequency of sessions and even the length of the hour, whether forty-five or fifty minutes, are usually determined by the analyst's own experience on the couch. Thus, because my sessions with Dr. Stevenson and Drs. R and L were fifty minutes long, its safe to assume that theirs were too, as are those of my patients; correspondingly, some of my colleagues go with forty-five as their analysts did with them. That's not so surprising if one considers the extent to which the process of identification takes hold (if we don't rebel) and why it is that we analysts, like children, tend to carry on the history of our own analyses as we become analysts ourselves (as if generating a family tree of analysts begetting analysts, all tracing back their heritage to Freud).

Whatever the defined length of the hour, most analysts agree upon the import of starting and ending on time, recognizing the centrality of maintaining boundaries and remaining within the established frame—something that some patients protest the most. Ending on time can be difficult for the analyst too, but it must be done, not only to create and maintain a safe space but also to affirm that the analysand is neither so ill nor so powerful as to be able to seduce the analyst to giving more (to mention only two fantasies that could be played out by bending the frame).

One patient whose fantasies of being closer to me lay at the core of her wish for me to 'bend' the rules and let her stay longer often asked me sarcastically whether I was afraid that "the psychoanalytic powers-that-be would take away my couch" if I didn't end an hour on time. In her previous treatment (which lasted over five years), Mrs. M's therapist had bent the rules in a variety of ways including giving her extra time, offering and scheduling double sessions (for which she charged of course), and exchanging favors or gifts with her—effectively persuading Mrs. M she was so damaged that she required more than anyone else.

At our outset, she tried the same tack with me: following a series of consultations in which she struggled about whether to work with me as opposed to someone more senior in the field, Mrs. M finally made what was a wrenching decision for her (to go against the authorities who had been so intimidating to her) and arrived for our first session with a present for me. It was a difficult moment: I knew how very sensitive and vulnerable she was, but I also knew how damaging her previous treatment had been and with the most gentle apology I could muster, refused her gift. As I had anticipated, she felt quite rebuffed even though she "understood" the reasons for my refusal. Fortunately, we had made a positive enough connection during our consultations (in fact an over-idealized one on her part) that she was able to start to explore the significance of her wish to give a gift, a major theme of her treatment as it turned out. Only by giving, she believed, could she provide the "glue" to sustain my interest in her. Much later, Mrs. M came to see that the prior treatment had exacerbated her image of herself as being damaged to the extent that she believed she had "created the monster" that had "forced" her previous therapist to bend the rules for her, replaying and reinforcing (as we later discovered) a pivotal childhood theme.

On the matter of the significance of maintaining the frame, I would also offer up my own experience as a patient. A few years into the analysis with Dr. Stevenson, when I was still feeling intensely possessed by and about him, he was five minutes late for a session, a stunning departure since he always began and ended exactly on time. I, who typically timed my arrival so that I'd have only a minute or two to spare (anything not to wait), rang the bell on the unlatched door, walked in, and sat down in the waiting room not even bothering to pick up a magazine. I instantly noted when our usual start time came and went and as one more minute passed, my vigilance turned to worry almost immediately superseded by a flood of anxiety—something had happened to him. But this quickly converted to burning anger that he was late, then to desperation that he had forgotten the appointment, i.e., me. Finally, my purgatory having lasted five real-time minutes long, Dr. Stevenson appeared and in his usual manner invited me in—without apology.

By that point I was suffused with indignation bordering on rage, mixed with shame at what felt like my overreaction and loss of control—not unlike the kaleidoscope of emotions that had overtaken me at the time of the Color War tennis match. In session, I said absolutely nothing for an uncharacteristically long time, even well after Dr Stevenson's quiet comment that I seemed so angry, I seemed to have withdrawn: could I talk about it? I seemed to be having a reaction to his lateness; was I punishing him back with my silence as well as my fury? Unknowingly of course, I was, although in fact I couldn't speak.

But he waited, and bit by bit I became emboldened to spell out what I had bottled up—the feelings of unimportance and abandonment that had been triggered by my having to wait, along with the smoldering rage I transferred to him as my father whose work came before everything else, yet more confirmation of the extent to which I had grown up feeling like an intruder and beyond the pale. Gradually in that session and the next I worked my way back to a level of trust, an illustration of the powerful effect of transference and a piece of analytic work.

That incident also embodies the answer to the common question of why analysts tend not to observe social amenities like apologizing for being late. An immediate apology might have suppressed my reactions, and that would have been the opposite of what treatment is about. If the analyst responds to some current reality, he risks bypassing what will emerge from the patient's past. And indeed, had Dr. Stevenson apologized, I undoubtedly would have accepted his excuse and the matter would have simmered or dead-ended there. The fact that he did eventually acknowledge his lateness is indicative of the shift from the day when the analyst almost never acknowledged anything and everything was attributed solely to the patient and his or her issues, as if the analyst did not exist.

That's exactly the way it was early in my treatment with Dr. L when one day I heard the sound of a baby crying as I sat in her waiting room. It had sounded so close that it seemed it might have been in the same apartment and so I mentioned it at the start of the session, curious of course, about whether it was hers. But without ever indicating whether or not she had heard it herself, Dr. L quickly interpreted that what I thought I heard reflected my wish for a baby. Nothing more. No matter what I said, Dr. L refused to validate my experience or my curiosity and instead kept focusing on my unconscious wishes for a child. Finally I gave in, and in keeping with the nature of that treatment, never addressed how misunderstood I felt.

What matters most about analytic sessions however, is the extent to which cumulatively they facilitate a deeper return to the past in the form of a full-blown transference, such that a psychoanalysis can become a journey with a beginning, a middle and an end—unlike a twice-a-week therapy, which, however useful, typically has a flatter curve. The patient who has gotten angry at a therapist on Monday may still remember on Thursday but the matter will likely have cooled or become more intellectualized than felt, depending on his or her particular defenses; the analysand who comes the next day and the day after, however, has a much greater opportunity to discover that he or she is (re)acting in the present to something familiar from the past.

Another example: Mrs. M, the same patient who challenged me about ending the hour on time, became enraged when she noticed that the ficus tree I'd had for years at the foot of the couch was dead. Of rather concrete mind at the time, she had often commented on the tree, certain that it thrived because I took such good care of it as she wanted me to take care of her although she continued to deny the parallels when I suggested them. One August when I was away the tree died, a victim of the heat, and on my return, Mrs. M, already distressed about the month's separation, became furious, convinced I would neglect her as I had the tree—just as her abusive mother had done to her. (During several crises in both her childhood and adolescence, the mother's passivity resulted in some serious injury to

Mrs. M which she had had to handle on her own, feeling both abandoned and abused.)

In the regression of the transference old feelings took over, and Mrs. M temporarily lost the over-idealization that had allowed her to trust me as the benevolent analyst who could be helpful to her. Inevitably, a number of times over the course of our work, she felt betrayed by something I said or did not say, did or did not do, and threatened to leave. But with repeated experiences of my tolerating and containing her attacks and rage and with interpretation, Mrs. M was able to regroup, until the cycle would begin anew requiring us to work things through again—a demonstration of how the here and now of transference and treatment proceeds.

This example also illustrates a key difference between traditional and contemporary versions of psychoanalysis: in the context of today's analyst's non-judgmental listening, tolerating, understanding, limit setting or holding, an analysand can come to feel emotionally re-parented in a benevolent way. I don't mean reparented literally, as though the analyst actually advises or acts the way a good-enough parent might have done: that's not the analyst's role. Besides, psychological change doesn't happen in that way; we can't undo the past. What I do mean is that over time, the experience with the analyst gradually helps diminish the volume of abusive, anxious, punitive, neglecting or over-indulgent parental voices dwelling inside (introjects), and ultimately allows a patient's own voice to emerge and flourish in a variety of ways, including as a more benevolent self-parental one.

Here's an example of what I mean, a difficult-to-illustrate intangible shift: one day on the tennis court, instead of falling over a familiar edge in competition with my husband, I found myself able to regroup. At the changeover in the midst of a close set, (6-5, my lead), my husband looked at his watch and asked me what we should have for lunch, implying that he was about to take control (as he has so often done); even though I was now more immune to his tactics (as I reminded him), in the next game I still missed two relatively easy returns, then double-faulted and lost that game which, of course, tied the set, prompting me to feel on some familiar angry and irrational edge.

But at the next changeover, I took a drink of water, wet my face and wrists with a corner of the towel and recaptured the stray hairs that had slipped from my barrette during the vigorous set; then when the barrette still didn't feel secure, I redid it firmly again and, with another sip of water, walked back onto the court ready for play. Strangely comforted and settled, I felt put back together in the way one might, I subsequently realized, after refueling at a mother's knee: she might adjust an article of clothing, put a band-aid on a sore, or even straighten one's hair with an affectionate touch.

I had been able to mother myself—the least and the best that I could do. Not only had my mood lifted, I looked forward to battling out the rest of the set and in this instance, did win. Of course, it doesn't happen all the time, but often enough for me to know that it represents a significant before and after. Other variations on that theme are even more subtle and to the onlooker, undoubtedly invisible. For example, given my husband's sometimes ability to pull me from side to side or my sometimes ability to make some spectacular 'gets' of my own (even if I do lose the point or game), instead of the familiar anger and humiliation, now I can often delight in my ability to have done as much and can laugh at the joy of the game. While I doubt that I will ever drop my racquet to applaud that point as my father might have done, the capacity to feel that joy represents an internal shift that fills me with the same wonder I feel when a patient begins to be freed up from repeating the patterns of an archaic self.

A woman who had been in treatment for over five years began a session with tearful wonder. Throughout much of our time together, she had struggled (in the transference) to ward off closeness out of her fears that I would suffocate or stuff her with my own intrusive longings and needs as her mother had done to her; over time we had discovered that her pattern with men had been a sadistic teasing dance of power and control that repeated her mother's behavior with her—there was no real closeness but victories (theirs or hers) or defeat (theirs or hers). Noting that the presence of a new man in her life was characterized by an intimacy and friendship she had never experienced before, commenting about the brittle angry armor she begins to relinquish with me and in her dealings with men, she wept as she said, "You have given me a great gift."

No doubt about it, psychoanalysis is an odd journey, a mix of the mundane and the sublime, and of course the sorrowful too. Sometimes it's hard to identify the fulcrum of change in the moment, sometimes the elements can be recognized only afterward in a cumulative sense. So perhaps an extended (and cherished) vignette from my work with Dr. Stevenson will convey what I mean.

I've already portrayed the first few years of that analysis as largely a vale of tears about my sense of exclusion and inadequacy and the degree to which I was consumed by thoughts and feelings about him. (A voluminous journal that I kept for about as many years testifies to that angst although it also chronicles the salient events of those years, my father's death, my family, work, the course of analytic training, etc.) But one day, at least five years into the analysis, on my way home I continued to replay a session that had left me feeling upbeat, even bemused, particularly the few moments toward the end during which I spontaneously and gleefully challenged Dr. Stevenson to a tennis match: "Name your time and place," I'd said.

I don't even remember what precipitated my tossing of that gauntlet except that I wanted to refute something he had said. No matter, the challenge just popped out—to which, in best compromise mode, Dr. Stevenson teasingly offered to take me up on it a few years hence. I immediately protested: this was hardly a fair counter-proposal since I'd be approaching my seventies by that time, too old to cover the court well, one of the best features of my game. Moreover, he was five years younger, not to mention that he was a man. But even then, he upped the ante and added, ". . . what's more, I'll play against you using my right hand." At that point, he had completely confused me.

Several years earlier, before I could fathom any kind of playfulness on my part or his (in session, in imagination or any place else), Dr. Stevenson had challenged my husband to a tennis duel: "Relay the message," he had jousted, "and tell him that I will play him using my left hand." Why had he made a point of that, I had wondered at the time? As the left-handed person I knew him to be (I'd seen him write), of course he would play with his left. But what I didn't know then was that he was ambidextrous and played tennis with his right!

What we had here was a stroke of psychological warfare at its best. For Dr. Stevenson to propose to play with his left hand was the equivalent of spotting my husband several points or perhaps games, a supreme expression of confident superiority. (This was becoming a maze that could daunt Theseus at his best.) But his offer to play me right-handed, in five years or whenever, was about something quite else—his acknowledgment of my competence and enhanced capacity to tolerate a fray. That is, in the arena of fantasy and daydream created by the analytic space, my analyst could and would play his best game against me. I also realized he felt I could and would do my best; occasionally, I even found myself entertaining the fantasy that perhaps, like me, under pressure, he would lose his cool. Clearly, I was making progress in the analysis.

How did I know Dr. Stevenson was an accomplished tennis player? How did I know his age? Certainly not because he ever told me. On the contrary: these are the very kinds of personal particulars usually withheld that an analysand, hungry for tidbits about an analyst, will search out. The age part was easy. Early in the analysis (in pre-Google days), I looked him up in a professional directory where I found his academic credentials, areas of specialization, institutional affiliations, and date of birth, which last placed me quite symmetrically between my husband (exactly five years older) and him. If being sandwiched between the two men led to a variety of fantasied scenarios, it mostly felt like a comfortable fit.

Tracking the tennis part was more complicated. Once I became an analytic candidate, I saw and heard the fairly prominent Dr. Stevenson at many of the colloquia and presentations so essential to the analytic community. On one occasion at which he was the main speaker (much to my mixed excitement and dismay), I listened as his colleague and friend Dr. Bevans introduced him, beginning with his professional accomplishments and winding up with a flourish: "...Dr. Stevenson is also a Renaissance Man, winner of tennis trophies, musician, and master of other diverse skills, including the patience to hit tennis balls with a novice with whom no one else is patient enough to play, me." A charming and humorous introduction often lacking at such scientific meetings, for my very own analyst, it was over-the-top.

In fact it blew me away, reminding me of my excluded state, deprived of the closeness of casual play and who knew what else (dinners, phone calls, casual conversations, weekends in the country, whatever easy access such a friendship might allow). And worse—although I already knew that Dr. Stevenson played tennis, the discovery that he won tournaments was a blow, yet another sign of his superiority and capacity for excellence, underscoring (in my mind) the very deficiencies that had brought me to treatment. Since then, I have wondered, or is it hoped, that Dr. Bevans might have been spoofing about his winning tournaments. But of course by that time, the reality of whether he did or didn't was irrelevant. At that time, Dr. Stevenson had more and was better at everything than I (in my mind of course).

I'm not even ashamed to admit that it took me weeks to recover from the despair with which I was stricken on hearing

Dr. Bevans' introductory revelations, in no small part because the despair swiftly metabolized into my too familiar sense of not measuring up and its corollary, my being excluded. If you haven't been there, I realize that such a pattern of reactions in a grown woman and competent professional may sound ridiculous. But ridiculous or not, it's one illustration of what can and should happen in an analysis, especially the way the power of the transference can take utter hold.

More ideally, that intensity deepens gradually, and that, as I've already described, is not how it happened with me. Sparked by the *coup de foudre* of Dr. Edwards's recommendation of Dr. Stevenson as "the best," my treatment actually began before I even consulted him since he so immediately became a version of my father. Thus it took no time for me to regress to the role of an outsider, sometimes a nuisance, sometimes an asshole (on a bad day), always potentially beyond the pale. (Not that at other times Dr. Stevenson hasn't represented aspects of the good-enough mother who holds and is in attunement with her child.)

I hated the separations between sessions, unbearable distances that he controlled, while my feelings of admiration and love intensified, creating even more longing on my part. In session, I feared being stupid (especially when it came to talking about my work), anticipated his criticism (it never came) and was easily humiliated by anything that might indicate I wasn't competent, didn't know enough, or could never be in his league. Even with the increase in the number of sessions (with its underlying unconscious fantasy that possession or perfection would grant me what I longed for), I could never belong fully to him or he to me.

Then too, I had become a psychoanalytic candidate and that community (beleaguered from the outside) is very small—at best familiar, at worst bordering on the incestuous—definitely a fertile playing field for sibling rivalries and oedipal dramas, including mine. Deprived as an analysand by the necessary boundaries between the personal and professional, no matter what I understood intellectually, I found it extremely painful to witness the fact that others had access to my analyst that I could not have.

Chief among those others was his wife whom I liked (also an analyst, her name appearing just below his in the professional directory) and with whom I inevitably came in contact at the institute with which we were both affiliated and where we were often in agreement when there was an issue under debate. For years into the treatment, despite Dr. Stevenson's best efforts to draw them out, I tried to keep my competitive feelings toward her on hold usually by displacing them, onto colleagues, friends, or other analysands who had direct contact with him. It was they who bore the brunt of my envy and ongoing sense of exclusion and loss, despite what had quickly become a five-times-a-week analysis that still didn't feel like enough—not for the daughter of a man who had felt excluded by the distance created by his work.

Many might well wonder, who in his or her right mind would undertake such a tortured experience and for so long? No one, probably, were it not for the hope and promise of getting to the other side, as indeed I very gradually did. In fact, it was on the day I mused fondly post-session about having teasingly challenged Dr. Stevenson to a tennis match and the reciprocal repartee that ensued, that I realized that our banter signaled the emergence of something new: in the intimate distance of the experience, in the process of being listened to and understood, I had been playful and *played* with Dr. Stevenson in the analytic space. To have become able to challenge someone I respected and loved instead of withdrawing, was a victory hard won and I felt a surge of wonder and love. Transference for sure, but at what point does it become the real thing?

mostly about omissions and consolidations

It may indeed be questioned whether we have any memories at all from our childhood: memories relating to our childhood may be all that we possess.

Freud, Screen Memories
(SE, Vol. III, p. 322)

When Nora was two, her sister Bridget (also called Delia or Dilly) was born, followed in 1889 by twin girls. At one or another of these births (accounts vary and there is no written record) Nora was sent to live with her maternal grandmother, Catherine Mortimer Healy. This was Nora's first exile and the one that most shaped her personality.

In leaving the crowded nest, Nora gained many material advantages. She probably had better food than was served at her mother's table, where there were so many mouths to feed. At her Grandmother Healy's, she enjoyed lemonade and currant cake, a piano, and pictures on the walls, which were decorated with holly and ivy at Christmas. Her grandmother was kind to her. When her best friend, Emily Lyons, left for America and Nora wept inconsolably, Mrs. Healy gave her a new pinafore to wear and sat her down by the fire with bread and butter. Michael Healy tried to cheer her up with a new pair of buttoned-up boots. Her grandmother also taught Nora (as she had taught Nora's mother) good table manners and the polite forms of speech. But Nora never forgave her mother for shutting her out.

Brenda Maddox, *Nora, The Real Life of Molly Bloom*

L ooking back at my past through the lens of psychoanalysis was a stunning experience for me if only because, by exposing the rigidity, loneliness, and limitations of the world in which I grew, it challenged my conviction that I had had an ideal childhood. It also countered the shame that had been gnawing at me ever since I fell apart in adolescence: what could possibly have accounted for things going so seriously wrong? After all, I had been well-fed and tended to and treated with respect by parents who loved me and always encouraged me to do the best I could. Of traumas there had been none—or so I thought.

Since then, in my work I have come across many who feel similarly shamed and bewildered, who have erroneously assumed (as I did) that a history of specific abuse or overt trauma is a necessary cause of damage to one's core being and sense of self. But now I know otherwise, having discovered that many seemingly benign acts of omission or commission during our formative years can impact negatively and profoundly on our sense of selves and that the *absence-of* can be as devastating as the *presence-of* too much. What I am describing is what psychoanalyst Masud Khan (a contemporary of Winnicott and Klein) identified as *cumulative trauma,* seemingly innocuous experiences over time that can become incrementally toxic to a developing child.

From this perspective, the farthest-reaching such experience of my young life derived from the decision of my parents to have me sleep in their bedroom until I was almost seven. The official explanation was that our two-bedroom apartment was too small to house our family, which at the time of my birth included not only my sister but my paternal aunt who had moved in at my father's insistence following the death of their mother several years before. Since my aunt and my sister were already sharing the second bedroom when I came along, my parents took me into their own, a reasonable intervention for those days on the face of it—but only the surface topography of a much more textured event.

For one thing, my unmarried aunt, a self-supporting teacher, could well have continued to stay in the apartment where she had moved with my newly widowed grandmother on the 4th Street side of our building several years before—close enough for comfort but far enough to allow for some separation. Instead her move crowded us in what was for those days and in that neighborhood, a luxurious apartment with two bedrooms, dining room, living room, and an eat-in kitchen as well. Asserting that space was less important than family loyalty, my father insisted that my aunt move in with us because of her spinster status although he also acknowledged that economics played a role—as a young lawyer starting out at the end of the Depression, money was scarce. And it is true that he did accept my aunt's financial contribution toward such extras as camp for my sister and me.

But I believe the governing dynamic was his inability to separate from his past, buttressed by a large element of unconscious guilt. Perhaps he could not allow himself to have more in the way of material comfort than his parents or to live more luxuriously than they did. Indeed, despite my mother's entreaties over the decades and several opportunities to move, my parents remained in the unfashionable neighborhood of my father's birth for well over thirty-five years, leaving it only when he was in his early sixties and the Lower East Side had transmuted into Alphabet City and drugs had overrun the streets.

Naturally, the sleeping arrangements affected us all in a variety of ways but as a young child they surely affected me at every developmental stage. Central among the psychological insults, to be in the parental bedroom most profoundly over-complicated the oedipal drama for me. Besides mixing the oedipal message (itself no small thing), it placed me in the midst of an untenable conflict between feeling special and chosen or feeling insignificant and left out. In that binary calculus, if I "won," then someone lost—my sister, my mother, or later my opponent on the tennis court—and I feared retribution; if I did not win, that is, if I lost, then I was excluded and alone.

In this calculus were surely the seeds of the competitiveness I disavowed so absolutely until and long after Dr. Stevenson first suggested that much of my behavior masked a competitive streak, his response to a Monday-morning lament about the past weekend's tennis with my husband and my general frustration about my game. I immediately parried back the suggestion that perhaps the competitive issue was his, not mine, yet another instance of the level of denial about my competitiveness, not just on the court but about almost everything else.

For a small child, who by virtue of developmental age would have been unable to tolerate ambiguity or ambivalence, the bedroom conflict was irreconcilable. It all too readily evolved into the unconscious paradigm that underlay the dynamics of my patterns on the tennis court, and as I would discover many years later, into the drama I played out in almost every area of my life. As soon as I would work myself into some place or position of success (that Color War match, progress with a particular patient, my graduation from analytic training when I spoke too long), I would unconsciously do something to compromise the achievement and rob myself of full satisfaction—usually subtle, nothing scandalous or shameful—something that would get me to feel excluded from or put out of the symbolic bedroom.

At the height of the intensity of my analysis with Dr. Stevenson, when I was grappling with the paradox of feeling both special and insignificant (originally in the bedroom, then in his office or at the institute to which he belonged), I came across Phyllis Greenacre's stunningly apt evocation of people, like me, who have been psychologically or physically marginalized, that is, excluded-in or included-out. Take your pick. Meteorites from theoretical space, those deceptively simple symmetries at once coalesced with the anguished hours that had been engulfing me, encapsulating the circumstantial ambiguity and emotionally poisonous currents that made me feel I could never win or fully belong. As in truth, as a child, I could not if I compared myself to my beautiful mother who had a place in bed with my father, just where a little girl often wants to be herself, although in an earlier phase, it is often the mother with whom the little girl wants to be or to merge.

Further, I was witness to the tantalizing and frightening mysteries my father and beautiful mother shared (the primal scene). And since my young thinking was still quite literal, the perceived action was over-stimulating and severely anxiety-provoking: whatever sexual activities went on between my parents could only seem violent to me, about being invaded and subdued, about annihilating, about hurting or being hurt, while memory of those primitive sounds and attendant images left indelible psychological traces largely of the inhibiting kind.

For my parents, nothing could have been further from conscious mind. Typical of their generation, they assumed that my sharing their bedroom would do me no harm, however inconvenient for them. As a small child in an orderly household I would have been put to bed long before my father came home and would have been asleep by the time they went to bed, and for the most part I guess I was. Delightful exceptions that I loved were those times my father would wake me as he was getting ready for bed by dropping a shoe or making some noise just to say hello before sending me back to sleep; being with him was already a rare treat and his waking me added to my excitement about him. (I do have a vague sense of my mother's disapproval but don't know whether it was because she was concerned that I would not go back to sleep or because she resented my presence in the first place. Probably both.)

Through reconstruction with Dr. Stevenson I learned about the degree to which those moments with my father established a baseline for the ease with which I could be teased (excited and pulled in) and then told to deny or suppress what I was feeling (by being a good girl and going back to bed). They also became harbingers of my association of danger with anything too intense, any such emotion as excitement or anger, positive or negative.

From almost every developmental vantage point, the very people whose role was to protect me had put me in a situation I simply could not manage safely on my own, and since they were so naive about its potential impact on me, they were unable to help me talk about, or cope with it. And in that tantalizing, frustrating, irreconcilable situation lay the roots of the uneasy sense of self I grew up with, at one and the same time special enough to sleep in the parental bedroom but never good enough to be in their bed. No wonder my grownup self struggled anxiously before I could even ask Dr. Stevenson to increase the number of my weekly sessions: could or would he make room for me, the insignificant child in the bedroom? Nor is it surprising that I spent the early years of my analysis in a state of agitation, never sure I could safely stay, never knowing how long would be long enough. Not surprisingly, that heightened sensitivity also surfaces in my work, particularly in my tendency to be overly flexible with patients when scheduling or changing appointments; to this day I go out of my way to find hours more convenient for them or to accommodate them with a make-up lest they think I do not care enough to let them stay.

Another consequence of my stint in the parental bedroom is my extreme sensitivity to subtle motion or sound, enough to create odd pockets of discomfort, sometimes even a sense of physical pain. For example, not everyone would require two layers of insulation between the marble lobby adjoining an office (mine) to ward off the laughter and trumpeting sneezes of the too-social doormen next door. On the tennis court, the same: the buzz of a plane, the approach of a car, or even the seasonal honking of the geese approaching our pond can cost me a point, a double fault, sometimes a set. And in session, even the slightest movement of Dr. Stevenson in his chair would unsettle me: was he restless? impatient? not interested in me? Until very recently, any motion would shut me down and several minutes would pass before I could resume talking, a pattern about which I was quite unaware until Dr. Stevenson pointed it out.

Finally, sleeping in my parents' bedroom taught me to block out what I unknowingly wished not to see, something too charged to confront. That such denial can actually obscure one's vision I discovered for myself after I, certain of my facts, agreed to the first of Dr. Stevenson's numerous bets—which I usually lost. In this instance the subject was the inadequacy and shame I sometimes felt with Dr. Edwards, the admired supervisor from whom I'd gotten his name. At some point, Dr. Stevenson suggested that perhaps he had become a father figure whose good opinion was essential to me, stirring my familiar anxiety that I'd never measure up. Emphatically not, I insisted, there was no similarity at all between my father and Dr. Edwards. Besides, I didn't want another father symbolically or any other way; the one I had was more than enough.

"No similarity at all, not even that Dr. Edwards wears bow ties?" Dr. Stevenson had asked. That, I replied, was ridiculous: in our entire year of face-to-face meetings to discuss my work, I had not once seen Dr. Edwards in a bow tie. But about this, Dr. Stevenson smilingly demurred. Incredulous that I could have missed such an essential detail, I looked forward to proving my point at a professional meeting several weeks away at which Dr. Edwards would be presenting a paper. Need I say it? Not only was he wearing a bow tie, but as he later confirmed, it was the only kind of tie he ever wore. I rest my case: transference and denial can obscure one's vision as well.

When I was almost seven, the sleeping arrangements finally changed. After years of waiting, the apartment next door became available and my parents broke through to combine it with ours. At first it seemed an expansive time as they created a new bedroom for themselves and a study for my father on the far side of the living room—almost a separate suite. At the start of the construction, the workers literally cut a hole in the wall and home from school for several days with a bad cold, I climbed back and forth between the two apartments delightedly as if from one world to another.

Soon pleasure turned to pain, my delight to near-agony as my breathing became labored and I gasped for air. My mother, who was in charge of such matters, was certain the construction dust was exacerbating my cold, (an assessment hardly consistent with the magnitude of my distress) but eventually she called in our pediatrician who diagnosed asthma, triggered by an allergic reaction to the cold compounded by the dust. Not even he whom I loved, little realizing that my affection was connected to the focused attention he paid me in those days of house calls, had the slightest inkling that the attack might have been induced by the stress of separation and change. In the midst of the family's shared anticipation and excitement about having more space, no one thought to imagine that the child who had been in the bedroom might feel she was being put out—which of course I was—but far too late to undo whatever psychological damage had been done. The event not only marked the end of an era but also signaled the beginning of my anxious reactions to change.

(A word about psychosomatic illness here. In keeping with the intimate relation between body and mind first recognized by

Breuer with Anna O and further conceptualized by Freud, some physical ailments such as paralysis, aphasia, a cough, even hysterical blindness can be symptomatic expressions of unconscious material that has been repressed. In the case of Anna O, this was confirmed when the symptoms disappeared as the repressed material, often of a sexual nature, came to light. But in order for such conflicts to take a physical form—become somatized—one must have a physiological predisposition to them. In the absence of such a genetic component, the symptoms will take non-physical forms, such as phobias or obsessive compulsive thoughts or acts.)

Eventually I outgrew the asthma, being one of the lucky ones for whom it was only the childhood kind, and at that, precipitated by guilt or anxiety about a major change—such as the time I was about to start at the private high school I had begged to transfer to from the local public school I attended with my sister (a senior). Utterly bored, I had been enticed by a camp friend's description of the small classes at her private school: she was learning to analyze literary characters, deconstruct poetry, experiment in the science lab, and play a variety of team sports, including tennis! But after I was accepted I found myself oddly conflicted about whether or not to go and "coincidentally" beset by an asthma attack, mostly from guilt related to my having opened a trap door to the competition I ordinarily shunned by daring to imagine I could be different from my sister or have more than she.

Until I changed schools, I had juggled the matter of differences between us by trying to follow in her footsteps, doing exactly what and as she did. Crazy as it might sound, I even strove to take as long with my homework as she, lest finishing too quickly signified that I had not worked hard enough. (I did not realize until years later that the sister I was copying was herself emulating my father's work-style—many drafts, many "struggles," and many long hours.)

I did, however, take real pleasure in our physical differences which clearly were not in my control. How could anyone blame me for growing taller or for having straighter, therefore better, hair? (My sister's was wiry and unruly like my mother's and had to be kept very short, a disadvantage about which they both despaired.) Or for having the freckles that captivated my father (my sister had none) and prompted him as I sat on his lap while he had his before-dinner-drink to seriously count them all, adding one or two more each time? Once on that lap I was allowed, even encouraged, to untie his bow tie which he would then retie, delighting in his ability to form it perfectly without aid of a mirror while seated.

And, most differentiating between my sister and me, she never slept in my parents' bedroom. Above all else, that made me feel as though I had been chosen over her. (In later years when I realized that most patterns have an inverse, I often wondered about the impact on my sister of her having been on the outside, as it were, from the start. Was that why she stayed too long in professional situations where she didn't quite belong, hoping to win out? Or why she assumed that she knew what was going on in other people's minds, how they felt about an experience, as if she had been present and part of it when indeed she was not?)

In the light of a healthier day, transferring to a private school doesn't sound like much of a conflict at all, especially since I had initiated the move myself. But the conflict was escalated not only by the guilt that made me feel more special than my sister but also by the threat of differentiation from my father, a loyal and proud product of the public schools. (Through letters and occasional visits, he devotedly kept up with his elementary school teacher Miss Bradley and she with him until she died. Among his papers, I came across her letter apologizing to him because illness prevented her from attending the occasion of his swearing in as a federal judge when he was about to turn fifty.) Fortunately though, when it came to academic endeavor, my father was uncharacteristically receptive to change and it was with his encouragement that I transferred and threw myself into the possibilities of learning with a sense of excitement that had been almost deadened in my local public school.

Still, on some level I felt I didn't belong. Most of my new class-mates lived uptown and had been together for years, so even though I was quickly accepted and participated in every aspect of school (even ran for office the next year and won), I was plagued by the familiar sense that I didn't quite fit in. It was all in my mind of course, just as it would be in college. Not until I fell out of the kingdom of my father could I begin to see that the child who had been excluded-in or included-out couldn't win, couldn't have more than anyone one else, that if she did, she would have to be punished, whether by losing on the tennis court or suffering an asthma attack. It is significant that the attacks actually ended when I left childhood behind—with the exception of a mild resurgence on my walks to work after I became engaged, when my anxiety about separating was finally for real.

Well, not quite. Just around the time I was putting the finishing touches on this manuscript, I found myself panting from any kind of exertion and experienced a sensation that someone was pressing slightly on my chest. Convinced that these were symptoms of lung cancer from which my sister had died about a year before, I was so terrified that I put off contacting my internist for weeks until I could procrastinate no longer and a chest x-ray came back indicating asthma instead.

Why now after so many years? For one thing, my husband and I were in the midst of a move from the apartment building in which we had lived for almost thirty years, for another I had only recently terminated the analysis with Dr. Stevenson. Despite the fact that both changes were by choice, they were major life events and inevitably entailed anxiety as well.

But why it never occurred to me that I might be suffering from asthma this time had less to do with denial than the form it took—no gasping for air, overt wheezing, or an allergic reaction to a cold—just constriction of airways that was detectible when I climbed stairs, walked vigorously, or my internist listened to my chest. Then too, as he ruefully reminded me, sometimes people at my stage of life develop asthma, even if they have never suffered from it before.

When, in the greater psychological sophistication of later years, I have thought about the multidimensional impact of my sleeping in the parental bedroom, I have wondered what might have impelled my father to invite a potential intruder into his marital relationship more than once—his sister into the apartment, me into the bedroom, later the secretary at work to whom he became intensely devoted (and she to him), upstaging what he seemed to have felt for my mother. Be it an educated guess or perhaps a wild leap, I believe that the propensity may have had its roots in my father's own familial history, a piece of a puzzle I learned of only as an adult.

When my paternal grandfather Abraham emigrated from Eastern Europe he left behind a wife and two children he planned to send for when he was able. Instead he married a woman he met here, (Fanny the grandmother after whom I was named), effectively abandoning the family that waited behind. While the fact that my grandfather actually had two women in his life was not such an unusual occurrence for those times, it's impossible not to think that it produced no fallout, let alone the half-siblings and numerous cousins it would take a genealogist to track down.*

I have no idea no idea when my father learned about his father's past, but knowing as I do now about the power of a secret (a suicide, a miscarriage, a traumatic death) to shape an entire family as well as the individual from whom it is kept, I wonder about its relationship to my father's habit of inviting another woman into his life. Was that rooted in some unconscious guilt about his father's betrayal with some corresponding need to repeat or repair it? Was it a major element in his need to be just and to follow the rules, perhaps a reparative reaction to the legacy of his father? After all, my grandfather had broken the law.

---

*Not so long ago I learned of the great resentment of some of those European-descended cousins, many of whom died in the Holocaust. In the universe in which I grew up my father had been admired and respected, but in theirs he was his father's son and as such the object of bitterness. Certainly they were not awed. Still, when my sister's daughter was being confirmed, we discovered that David Posner, the officiating rabbi, was descended from the family left behind. With this, a rapprochement that had begun after the war when my father helped some of the surviving cousins who emigrated here, continued to grow. It was Rabbi Posner who conducted the funeral service for my father and eight years later, for my mother as well.

In connection with this matter of family secrets, I think of a patient, Alison, whose mother died suddenly when she was two. When her father married a family friend soon afterward, the new couple simply substituted a new mother for the original without ever acknowledging either the existence or the death of Alison's own mother in what was presumably a well-intentioned effort to spare the child (and perhaps themselves) pain. All traces of Alison's biological mother (photographs, clothing) were erased; nor was there any mention made of her. It was as though there had been no loss to mourn. Only thirty years later, after her stepmother died and her father revealed the truth, did Alison come to understand her despair in the face of any separation or parting, her excessive anxiety about sudden disaster striking her children, her uncontrollable weeping at a film about loss, or the emotional storms that seemed to strike her from nowhere. Only then, as an adult in therapy, could Alison begin to disentangle her ever-present fears of catastrophe or loss; she also discovered the unconscious rage she felt about the betrayal, so much of which originated in a past she supposedly could never remember, let alone know about.

I am reminded also of Rachel who began treatment with me when she was thirty-three, the age at which her mother had died after a brief illness when Rachel was five. Like Alison's, her father married a family friend who soon adopted Rachel, but not before adding to the conflict and guilt of a little girl old enough to remember the mother she had lost by asking Rachel whether she'd like a new one. While the efforts her parents made to erase Rachel's mother were not as absolute as those that Alison's parents made, there were no questions or answers here either, no talking or weeping, nothing to help Rachel cope with her stupendous loss: photo albums were "lost," reels of film disappeared, silence substituted for memory. The child who would become my patient became frozen in psychic time, captive of the fantasy that she had somehow caused her mother's death, unconsciously awaiting her return. Feeling irreparably damaged by the irrevocability of her destructive power, Rachel was unable to undertake anything productive in work or in love.

In this limbo of loss and guilt, Rachel was convinced that she would die at the same age as her mother; in fact she longed to, hoping on some level to rejoin her in that way. But when she survived the critical year, having been denied both catastrophe and reunion, Rachel was able to undertake the arduous tasks of separating from the dead mother with whom she had yearned to merge and thawing the life she had put on hold. In a fairy tale, such an awakening can come about with the kiss of a prince; in real life it can require a great deal of therapeutic work. It has taken Rachel years to mourn her original loss, to recover from the betrayal of acquiescing to her biological mother's "replacement," and to process the added damage of having had her biological mother denied.

Since my father's experience with his father's abandonment of his first wife was not direct and certainly did not entail a crucial loss for him, I feel quite certain that he was less affected than Rachel or Alison who were first in the line of fire. For unlike either of them, my father had the kind of confidence about his place in the world that often is a by-product of being a favorite child—a position he shared with Freud, who wrote of it: "If a man has been his mother's undisputed darling, he retains through life the triumphant feeling, the confidence in success, which not seldom brings actual success along with it."

There is no doubt that Freud was treated as special. Always a serious student, when he complained as an adolescent that his sisters' piano practice was distracting him from his studies, the piano was removed! But unlike Freud, my father denied that he had been the favorite and insisted that his mother treated all her children with even-handed love and care (which claim my aunt contradicted), just as he and my mother did my sister and me. (Claiming and believing that they treated us equally and fairly, my parents remained oblivious to the deeper truth that is at the heart of sibling rivalry and its derivatives, envy and competition, those tributaries of my chronic guilt about, and terror of, feelings I wasn't supposed to have).

By contrast, my own sense of specialness as a child was based primarily on being the daughter of an exceptional man and all that flowed from that. Elaborated and complicated by the ambivalence engendered by being included-out of the parental bedroom, specialness was double-edged for me: it reinforced my feeling of differentness, which, however distinguishing, further compounded my isolation from my peers.

Even geography played a role: we lived in the only apartment building around, a universe apart from the square blocks of worn tenements and stoop-brownstones that surrounded it, only a half-block west from the one where my father had been born and raised. Yet for all his devotion to family or place, my father never took us to reminisce, to point out the actual building his parents owned, neither upstairs where he and the family lived, nor the saloon downstairs his parents ran and where he and his brother helped out. Then too, my mother remained ambivalent about the neighborhood to which she'd moved with her marriage, undoubtedly incorporating her own mother's unhappiness that she had left the upscale part of Brooklyn where they lived for the Lower East Side, presumably a step down instead of up. Except for those comfortable times I accompanied my mother to shop for vegetables at the stand run by Jenny, the buxom Italian widow who resided over a tiny alcove diagonally across Avenue A on Third Street, we never explored south of Houston Street, where surely the smell of pickles and sauerkraut emanating from barrels or the bustle of shopkeepers selling their wares might have given me more sense of place.

But if we did not belong to the Lower East Side, we also didn't belong to the uptown world where my father's colleagues and friends lived. An exception was Louis (Louie) Lefkowitz (later Attorney General of NY State) who lived on the Fourth Street side of our building, although here too, ambiguity reared its head. According to my parents, that side was less desirable than ours since it faced north, unlike ours which faced south and east and was flooded with sunlight all day long. (Old habits die hard: to this day, apartment or office, it is essential for me to have sunlight for the better part of a day.)

Like my sister (and my father and aunt before us), I went to the local elementary school which was half way down the block toward First Avenue where the sounds of the "El" rumbled intermittently through the classrooms all day. In those days viewed positively as a crucial piece of the melting pot for children of immigrants in their transition to the new world, even the public school experience differentiated me: unlike most of my classmates whose mothers accompanied them, I didn't even have to cross a street to get to school and by first grade was proudly going back and forth on my own. (At the time, I didn't understand that there might be a difference between need or want, and certainly didn't recognize that my pride masked some sense of deprivation created by my mother's absence, or that it might have had a negative impact on me.)

The other mothers, mainly of recent Eastern European or Italian descent, all seemed to be heavy-set, dark-clothed and older looking than my mother—yet another set of contrasts that set me apart. I could go on with examples, for among the many yardstick comparisons by which one comes to measure oneself as a child, everything of mine seemed not the same as that of everyone else. But if my feeling different sometimes meant feeling better than those to whom I compared myself, it also suffused me with a sense of inadequacy since none of it came from own accomplishments.

My mother was beautiful and slim, my father was a professional, they were the only ones (it seemed to me) who read The New York Times or subscribed to The Nation and The New Yorker; most other neighbors read The Mirror or The Daily News. Also, unlike the other mothers, mine was rarely at home when I arrived for lunch or after dismissal at 3 o'clock which I then saw as positively differentiating her from the other mothers around. Only in later years did I connect those omissions to her general unavailability or the variety of ailments that would intermittently send her to bed: a bad cold that turned into hacking bronchitis, menstrual cramps that felled her, frequent migraine headaches that wiped her out. On the one hand they all made me miss her; on the other, they made me feel like a nuisance or an intruder especially when I needed or wanted something from her, especially her company. And although I didn't recognize the origins for the longest time, my mother's succumbing to her ailments as readily and often as she did, produced in my adult self a horror of being sick (of being like her), the primary reason I've often refused to take to my bed even when feeling ill.

Among scant memories, I recall that my mother wasn't there on the day I stormed home from the first day of first grade, angry that my teacher hadn't yet started to teach us to read. I complained to Anna the cleaning woman, who comforted me instead and by the time my mother arrived, my sense of urgency had faded; with her reassuring laugh that we would undoubtedly start learning to read in the next few days, she dispatched my concern and consigned my impatience to a charming anecdote.

My desperation about reading (a harbinger of my lifelong pressure to excel) was mainly about wanting my father's attention and approval, more accurately, about wanting to be like him and do what he did. In fact I was so eager that I memorized a page of a primer belonging to my sister which I proudly "read" to him as I sat on his lap while he had his before-dinner-drink. But my sister would have none of it: recognizing my pretense ("You can't really read, you only have it memorized"), she quickly reduced me to tears. Soon pretense became the real thing: one day I was struggling with a list of words beginning with the letter "t" frustrated by my inability to distinguish *than* from *that*, the next day came recognition without effort. I was hooked and off running. Insights can be like that too.

---

[*]As these sibling things go, my sister showed remarkable restraint. Being the elder and having lost so much with my birth, she rarely took out her anger or disappointments on me.

Even such pockets of escape as reading further isolated me from my classmates, none of whom became friends in the full sense of the word. Friendly, but never friends. Lila, for example, had a small scar from chicken pox on her forehead that her mother would conceal each morning by moistening a strand of Lila's hair before sending her off to school, twining it into a spit-curl and pressing that onto her forehead with spatulate thumb. (As if in a photograph, I can see it to this day, curl under spatulate thumb.) After school, spit-curl intact, Lila and I would sometimes try to amuse ourselves in her father's furniture store above which the family lived, operating the machine that made buttons to hold tufted cushion fabrics in place; we never played games of any kind, not even hopscotch, potsy or the ubiquitous jump-rope to which so many of our contemporaries were addicted and at which they became correspondingly adept.

Phyllis, another classmate, lived two floors below us in the same line as ours; her birthday was one day before mine, a sort-of similarity that we warily shared. Like me she was proud of her father, a self-made businessman who had established a well-known chain of mens' clothing stores; I however, already convinced that being a professional was in the higher order of things, could not understand her pride. Nor could I relate to her overt competition with me, about fathers, birthdays, or anything else. To my dismay, she insisted on comparing report cards (usually a draw) and also contended that her lessons at the Third Street Settlement Music School were superior to mine with Miss Chasins, a private teacher whom I adored. I may have played more musically (an accurate perception) but Phyllis was learning theory and harmony and scorned my ignorance about sonata forms and fugues, to which I was indifferent at the time.

Our uneasy friendship came to an end when I was about ten. Phyllis had come upstairs one day so we could do our homework together and afterward initiated some mild sex play in the form of "you be the doctor and I'll be the nurse": this consisted of our examining one another's bodies, bared to the waist. Other than my scared excitement (quickly suppressed) at the sensation of her hands on my bare chest, I don't remember having any other reactions to our play. But several weeks later I terminated the relationship in a bizarre way for reasons I could neither fathom nor fight off: I had borrowed Phyllis's notebook to catch up on some school work I'd missed and after diligently copying down the math problems without looking at her answers, just before returning it, I pencilled in, in very very small letters in the margin of one of the pages, "I hate Phyllis N."

The writing was barely perceptible but I knew it would be found out. And it was. Several hours later, Phyllis's irate mother called me downstairs to demand that I explain why I had written the hateful words. But other than mumbling an apology, I couldn't answer what had possessed me or why. How does one explain impulsive behavior, especially when one hasn't even a clue that the deed was connected to guilt about the excitement generated by the sex play of several weeks before? But I never played with Phyllis again; to all intents and purposes, I had killed the relationship off. (That was one way of dealing with temptation; similarly, during adolescence, anorexia would accomplish the same for my more overtly sexual desires).

My parents had no notion of any of this. Running counter to my essential loneliness was their take and that of their friends, that I was an exceptionally amenable and exuberant child. To a large extent it was mine as well, until puberty hit at the too early age of ten, when I was uninformed and unprepared. Nothing about my period seemed right, from the wretched moment I discovered the blood (a sign of damage I was sure) to an episode at school when I asked to be excused because of my cramps and my sixth grade teacher thought I must be fabricating—how could I possibly have my period since she deemed me too young? This added to my sense of humiliation since my "conduct" on all report cards, like my subject performance, had always been graded "Excellent". Beyond that, getting my period way before the norm of thirteen or fourteen for those days singled me out, depriving me of a confidant or friend who could commiserate with me, exacerbating my sense of separateness and bringing with it a real sense of damage and shame about myself. Compounding all was the fact that I had skipped a grade and was a year younger than my classmates which yet again differentiated me.

Intuitively, I knew that my mother would be upset (and she was), so I concealed the news from her for several days and went instead to my sister who reassured me and told me what to do. Whether my mother's distress had to do with how young I was, the fact of my coming of age or both, it undoubtedly mirrored her discomfort with her own period which quickly became my own. For years I suffered excruciating cramps which, to my amazement, completely disappeared soon after I began treatment with Dr. R and discovered how ambivalent I was about being a woman (read being like my mother). That insight also ushered in a quite enlightening introduction to the power of the therapeutic process and the relationship between body and mind. Later, when the menstrual-like cramps returned with the onset of labor, I welcomed them as necessary components of the process of giving birth as indeed,

I mourned the loss of my period when it signaled the end of my child-bearing years.

Years later, when I understood more about dynamics and displacement, it surprised and relieved me to realize that what often seemed to me anger on the part of my mother, was more likely a reflection of her feeling upset and a reaction to her sense of helplessness to effect change. But in the matter of my getting my period, I interpreted her reaction as displeasure or possibly disappointment with me—in retrospect, another instance of how not-attuned she was—to herself or to me.

A representative memory of the solitary, shamed child I was underneath the happy persona my parents saw: at the age of six or seven I stand alone in front of our building, 3rd Street deserted at an early morning hour. From the depths of my pocket I pull a small cardboard container, cautiously remove a tightly coiled red paper roll and nest it securely within the small metal cap gun I have in hand. Surreptitiously first, then surrendering caution to the bravura of sound, I shoot the caps slowly until the reel is gone (twenty, thirty, or more, I have no idea how many). Strange delights mixed with discomfort: I loved the smell of sulphur that lingered long after, the very same as the residue from the matches my mother would strike to light her cigarettes. Still, in the sharp divisions of my childhood world, guns, like penises, were only for boys; my desire, seemingly forbidden but irresistible, intensified my growing sense of shame.

Other pleasures were essential: I sucked my thumb intensely at bedtime until one night when I was nine or ten, without any previous warning, my mother told me it was time to stop. "Big girls don't do that," she said, and good girl that I was, I immediately quit, suppressing my one dependable comfort and turned instead to the solace of books. Although every one in the household read, it seems to me that I discovered reading on my own and I'm quite certain that no one read to me at any age. In this cozy universe, I would get lost for afternoons on end, curled up in an armchair opposite the green-steepled church whose bells marked the hour, eating frozen chocolate-covered marshmallow twists that cracked between my teeth. (The contemporary look-alikes taste the same, but in the intervening years, alas, someone has changed the formula and they refuse to crack—another confirmation of the impossibility of ever fully recapturing the past.)

Soon reading took over as the passion of my life. I have no idea who introduced me to the public library opposite Tompkins Square Park, but I clearly remember my mostly solitary walks after school to take out the maximum of four books which I promptly consumed, returning a few days later for another round. Not even a dangerous encounter when I was around nine or ten could get in the way. My first direct experience with anti-Semitism occurred one rare time when I was walking home with a classmate from the library with my usual pile of books. It was also my first exposure to my own cowardice, which added a confusing dose of shame to the threat from the four or five neighborhood boys who encircled us. Looming huge, they menacingly accosted us with snowballs and ordered, "If you're Jewish, stay behind. If you're not, you can go." Unhesitatingly my classmate capitulated as she shook her head in denial and isolated, so did I, and we proceeded home without discussion of what had just occurred. Amazed that the gang accepted what seemed our obvious lies, I've sometimes wondered whether they were harmless all along, perhaps only excited by the inherent power of threats and not the prospect of deeds? I simply don't know.

World War II was underway and while I was too young to follow global strategies, amidst the domestic particulars of rationing, blood drives, posters cautioning silence, sweaters for servicemen knitted by a community group organized by my mother, I was certainly tuned into its implications and the sense of mortality implied, especially for those of us who were Jewish. Nevertheless, I continued my excursions to the library undeterred until reading for pleasure fell victim to my self-imposed pressure to concentrate on getting good grades, first in high school and then in college, where the seriousness of academic endeavor precluded for me the possibilities of play.

Resonant still are the long afternoons I spent with Nancy Drew and Cherry Ames on her path from student to full-fledged nurse or the assorted ballet dancers and women doctors whose stories I read and reread. I discovered *The Secret Garden* and *Mary Poppins* on my own, initially indignant, then awed by, the quirky governess's refusal to follow rules. I can still taste my anticipation on the day I was home sick from school and begged my mother, about to do her errands, to bring home *Mary Poppins Comes Back,* the just published sequel that I had been feverishly awaiting. What a felicitous coincidence of timing to command the universe (my mother) and devour a favorite, both from the comfort of my bed.

I found Dickens, O. Henry, and Horatio Hornblower at home, standing on the piano bench to reach the entire sets on a high shelf in the living room; I alternated the classics with comic books, gulping the unworthy latter with mild shame at the same time as I feverishly awaited the arrival of a next installment at the candy store down the block. My reading, an eclectic mix, was uncensored and I knew my parents approved. Although my mother would occasionally ask me why I didn't go outside to play (echoing the wise mother in *Ferdinand the Bull*, the original of which I still have), I also firmly recall the praise in her voice when I overheard her "complain" to a friend about my voracious reading habits; her pride added to my pleasure, although having a way to be like my father transcended even that.

I remember also my three-day immersion in *Gone With the Wind*, a marathon one summer weekend through which I raced nonstop to the end. I was fascinated by its passion and drama, especially when compared to the sterility of the history texts that bored me at school, equally fascinated if also confounded by the devastation of war or the madness of firing a first shot. I was impatient at the mysteriously different romance of Melanie and Ashley and filled with unbearable gloom that the tempestuous one between Scarlet and Rhett might end with their remaining apart.

Somewhat abashed that I was unable to conjure up my own version of what happened afterward (the conflict between reality and desire), I wrote for help to Margaret Mitchell, who wrote back through her secretary to say that she thought her readers ought to be able to figure it out for themselves. Many years later, on reading Mitchell's obituary, I was amused to learn that I was one of thousands who had asked the same question about Scarlett and Rhett and received a similar answer. Today, knowing as I do about the patterns people tend to replay, I think it likely that they would get back together again. Not to live happily ever after, but because something in each of their natures would compel them into a dance of attraction, rejection and pain, as it so often does in the patients with whom I work.

Except to mention the correspondence with Mitchell which my father would have encouraged (he was an inveterate letter-writer who often hand-penned thank-you notes in response to thank-you notes and urged us to do the same), I did not talk to either of my parents about the book. And I certainly did not talk to them when things took a more complicated turn as I read the first volume of Farrell's *Studs Lonigan* trilogy, which mesmerized and sickened me at once with its graphic sexual language and content. (I can still feel the waves of unease stirred by the word "titillated," which I encountered there for the first time and dutifully looked up.) Still, I read it all the way through, then indignantly threw it away—serious business for someone reared in a household that respected, even revered, books—but a measure of my terror of the possibility that any of the sexual content might pertain to me.

Since it's not unusual for adolescents to hold back much, if not most everything from the adults in their lives, the fact that there was no conversation between my parents and me about one or another book was probably age-appropriate. What was noteworthy and what I wish to underscore here, however, was the uniform absence of any discussion in our household, other, of course, than that pertaining to my father's work. Over time the cumulative silence left me locked in my own circumscribed world, reinforcing my sense of inadequacy and the attendant guilt and shame. Because I was unable to negotiate the conflicts that are the hallmark of adolescence (both exigencies and opportunities), a few years later, they would capsize my internal world.

Once again I have vaulted ahead of myself and am long overdue in retracing my steps and focusing on the path that opened up thanks to the therapeutic work I undertook with Dr. R. After college I decided to become a teacher and although the decision instilled some confidence that my life could take some direction away from the world of my father, it was a conflicted, even a tormented one. Although I was excited by the opportunities teaching offered me to bridge the intellectual and emotional parts of myself and in the process, to help young adolescents do the same, despite the value placed on learning in our family (compared to being a doctor or a lawyer) it seemed that to be a teacher was somehow lesser in the order of things, not to mention so much lower on the pay scale.

Still, to be responsible for the intellectual and emotional well-being of young lives had tremendous appeal: it dovetailed with my exhilarating experience as an apprentice at the Shady Hill School in Cambridge, which opened me up to the possibilities of learning and making connections; it also confirmed my expectation that learning to teach would be about learning to learn. I resolved the conflict by identifying with my father's conviction that money was inconsequential, that what mattered was love of, and pride in, one's work.

Yet once I left teaching and the security of a fixed salary scale, the matter of money would become exponentially complex. For years, charging a fee for my services filled me with unease, as though fulfillment through work should have been enough. Moreover the attitudes that I had internalized toward money collided with the functional realities of my field, in which setting and maintaining a fee help define the boundary between the personal and the professional, an essential part of the analytic frame.

Even without the legacy of my father, the whole question of fees in the analytic setting is no easy one. As a professional, obviously one does have to set a value on one's time, a mix that incorporates training, experience, the going market rate, and of course one's sense of worth. But what could be more paradoxical than a process that begins as a business arrangement but soon becomes charged with the currents of transference, be they of love or of hate? Even such a reality-based act as lowering one's fee can compound the ambiguities for a patient who might feel grateful to the very person who has, in the transference, the potential to turn into an object of hate or despair. That patient might be unable to express anger, another might read the accommodation as an indication of specialness or see it as a kind of stealing, another might pay exactly on time rather than risk punishment, while someone else might pay late by way of testing patience or love.

Nor are those who pay a full fee necessarily immune. Freud once commented that he wished he could treat a very wealthy patient without charging her—she was so convinced it was only her money that made her of interest to him. But he did not. To see her without charging would have violated the boundaries and could have created another kind of issue or guilt. Alas, most especially in psychoanalysis, there are no formulas about matters pertaining to money except to anticipate that they will inevitably become grist for the analytic mill—and have—consistently enough to make me long for the simplicity of my father's precepts regarding money. How I have envied his capacity to practice them without succumbing to the messy actualities.

For all that my father was parsimonious when it came to spending on himself (allowing need but not desire), he was instinctively generous with my sister and me.* Often when my mother took us shopping to buy clothes and we couldn't decide which of two dresses to keep, she would suggest that we bring them home to model for my father in his study after dinner to let him decide; invariably, he would suggest that we keep both, which of course, delighted my sister and me. Only later did I wonder why my mother could not have done the same, especially in later years when she became more and more unable to give, despite the fact that money was more available, not less. This was something my sister and I often complained and consoled one another about. Now of course, I wonder how much of my mother's constrained withholding was economically driven and how much was about the cumulative emotional deprivation that she, like my sister and me, experienced over the years of living with a man who did or could not take attention or time away from his work.

---

*There was certainly no room for greed in my father's scenario and I remember learning a corresponding, if humorous, punishment for mine: during the War, I stashed away as much scarce Fleer's Bubble Gum as a whole week's allowance would buy on the day our local candy store got its rare supply (each piece individually wrapped with a cartoon)...only to discover that the cache I had secreted away in my top bureau drawer had become rock-hard long before I could chew it all.

Although I had always been certain that I did not want to be a lawyer, in other ways, not only in matters of money, I continued to identify with my father. For instance, soon after I returned to New York I began walking back and forth to work and on weekends, I resumed playing tennis at those same courts in the Bronx where he had pitched the balls to me as a six year old. In a notable shift from my adolescence, I even acknowledged that tennis might have some social usefulness since my partners often asked me out, although *partners* is something of a misnomer because I still avoided sets, rallying with men who were warming up for their regular games: it was the familiar compromise; it gave me the sun and the sweat without the competitive threat. Then, when I relented and did date, to my regret, all too often my tennis partners were lawyers, so I was never sure whether they were interested in my father or me.

And that in turn tended to make me feel uncomfortable and small. I also felt that I had nothing of value or interest to talk to them about, a condition not limited to, but exaggerated when I went out with lawyers. Ever since I first started dating, I was so certain that I wouldn't have anything to talk about that I used to make a list of topics beforehand, a strategy that worked well enough to keep my worry down and get me going. But one evening, in those long-ago days when dates picked one up at home before going out, while entertaining one who was waiting for me, my father unknowingly stole my lines, exhausting my entire list. I was furious at him for I certainly had no idea then that he too had difficulty knowing what to talk about with anyone outside his sphere, certainly not an adolescent or college male. Although I did get past this inhibition somewhat with my boyfriend at college, I never felt comfortable being myself with or without a date.

Until, much to my amazement, in my mid-twenties, I fell in love with and married a man who was not a lawyer (intentional on my part) but who had never held a tennis racquet in his hand (unintentional). That he was not a lawyer was a source of great relief, if also mild apprehension; that he was not a tennis player gave me pause but it counted far less than finding someone who would not be wedded to his work. Besides, he seemed genuinely interested in me and attentive enough in our first encounter to have noted my seriousness about tennis to ask when we met again the next day whether I would mind missing my regular Saturday morning game to go sailing with him and some friends. Was he kidding? Would I mind? Captivated by his invitation, I not only agreed to relinquish my morning of tennis but managed to suppress my proclivity to sea sickness (heir to the car sickness I suffered as a child) and without a moment's hesitation, said "Yes." (Alas, that proclivity did win out and I spent most of the day diving into freezing water off a gently rocking boat on a becalmed day in preference to staying on board and wanting to die.) But even that did not deter—me or him.

Besides, he was handsome, had a gentle, teasing sense of humor and seemed to have come from a universe quite disparate from mine. His childhood, lived alternately in Brooklyn and Jerusalem, cast him in a foreign light and at the age of twenty-nine he had not yet settled on a profession, in marked contrast to my father who knew from childhood what he wanted to do. This non-lawyer had worked in fields ranging from navigation (as in aerial) to geology (as in roughnecking for oil), which unlikely variety exerted a fascinating and formidable pull on me.

Here was a man who embodied the possibility that I could free myself further from the weight of the rules and injunctions that had become so much a part of myself, that I might have a life different from that of my mother and father. Although my father frequently acknowledged his love for my mother and us, everyone and everything else felt secondary to his work and I did not want to take second place in my marriage to anyone or anything else.

The chemistry between us was so strong, there was no turning back the process set in motion one hot, sunny morning in August when the Paul Newman look-alike standing next to me as I paused for a red light en route to work asked, "Excuse me, don't you work at McGraw-Hill?" At the time I did, during what was to be a brief interlude between teaching jobs—as did he, between geology and whatever would come next—and he had noticed me on my morning treks north. As the light changed, we fell into step with one another and continued walking and talking our way up to 42nd Street where McGraw-Hill then was located. By the time we covered the remaining mile or so (the shortest one I'd ever walked), we had discovered that we lived within two blocks of one another, regularly walked to work, were both at McGraw-Hill temporarily while trying to figure out what to do with our lives—all of which created a sense of inevitability about our coming together. (It was more than enough for me to have determined to look for, and to find him the next day and for him to have then asked me out.) As we reached the big green building and prepared to part, he to an annex on Forty-first Street I hadn't even known about, I experienced a surprising and disproportionate sense of loss. Would I ever find him again? And turned to ask, "I'm sorry, but I don't even know your name," (the exact words, uninspired but to the point). Even more surprising was the unexpected surge of relief when he answered, "It's Cohen, Dan Cohen." (Jewish, I thought. I could marry him.)

Call it fate or a pickup (as my husband still prefers), the memory of our meeting still gives rise to a shiver of excitement and romance. The gravitational pull was so strong that we never really had a second date, and it didn't take long before I quelled whatever trepidations I had about the uncertainty of marrying someone without a profession or a life without tennis in favor of the prospect of a future with a man who seemed committed to sustaining a relationship with me and with our children once we had them.

Still, after all these years, I can recapture my anxiety about our differences and the danger of deviating from a "correct" path. The absence of a passion for an identifiable profession made my husband-to-be paradoxically both an object of desire (the opposite of my father) and an object of concern: meaningful work definitely mattered to me as a fundamental source of self and self-worth and to a large irrational extent, father/professional/lawyer/hard work were still locked into the same atomic configuration for me.

In truth, I wanted it all. I wanted my husband to have a successful career but I did not want it to consume him, not at the cost of our marriage taking second place. And more. I wanted what seemed missing in my parents' relationship to one another and to me: I wanted him to take care of me and to be active in our family life—all reflections of the quite universal human tendency to try to undo or to repair the past. Indeed, I am convinced that without the intervention of treatment, I would have married some workaholic version of my father with the unconscious fantasy of making the ending come out differently, that is, of getting him to change as a sign of his love for me.

As I often say to patients who are caught in their own versions of that bind, such fantasied scenarios don't usually work out, if only because re-enacting the past requires us to pick someone enough like the original that he, like my father, would be impervious to such change. (The adult who has been abused as a child is the classic example: unconsciously drawn by the familiarity and motivated by the fantasy of repair or gaining love, he or she may choose the kind of partner who will actually recapitulate the abusing situation instead of avoiding it.) This is not to suggest that I believe I had control over my destiny once I realized what had been missing, but rather to point out that our human struggles to negotiate the present are so often attempts to renegotiate the past.

And why I firmly believe in the potential of psychoanalysis to free us from the ghosts who haunt us and imprison us. For those of us who are fortunate (as I believe I was), it confers the opportunity and sets the stage for us to re-experience and to repair, in the contained safety of the treatment setting, some of the conflicts/wishes/losses/traumas that define our individual selves and eventually to work them through—in large part by gaining a different perspective on our earliest days. Labor-intensive for sure, to some a luxury or even an indulgence, I have no doubt that for many, psychoanalysis is a necessity for "soul to clap its hands and sing."*

Naturally, it wasn't just chemistry and excitement that propelled me into marriage with a man who was neither lawyer nor tennis

---

*Yeats, "Sailing to Byzantium"

player but the freeing up of possibilities, and that was the wonderful gift of the treatment that followed my falling apart. Still, I was not so buoyed by being in love that the prospect of further separation from my family (real and psychological) didn't stir considerable anxiety in me. It's not all bad—anxiety, that is. It can be a signal or manifestation of conflict and if one can tolerate it and track it down to its source, one can be the richer for grappling with it. And by then, I could and did.

My own anxiety was compounded by my parents' quiet disapproval of my choice. For one thing, there was little in their frame of reference to enable them to evaluate my boyfriend by any standard beyond the monumental fact that he was not yet settled in work. (That he had fought in the Israeli War of Independence gave him a certain cachet but not enough to make up for absence of a defined career.) For another, in my worry over whether they'd like him, let alone endorse our plan to marry, I sprang the news on them far too abruptly, trying it out first on my mother in the kitchen as she was preparing dinner and inducing so negative a reaction that we both ended up in tears. Five minutes later, hoping for something better, I told my father without waiting for him to have more than a sip of his before-dinner-drink. He greeted the news with a frown (oh, how I longed for a smile) and a barb, "What makes you think that this one is any different from all the others?"

He was referring, of course, to the number of relationships I'd had during and since college (which he undoubtedly attributed to my instability—just one among a number of critical judgments of me he never actually rendered aloud), whereas he had only ever been interested in my mother whom he met when he was twenty-two and she was seventeen, a year too young for law school (intending to bypass college as my father did). Instead, she took what was to have been a temporary job as his secretary and stayed on. And on. I don't know at what point they began to date, but I do know that after five years(!), she went to work for someone else, prompted by her authoritarian father who was impatient at my father's inability to tear enough of himself away from work to commit to her; only when her father died and my father paid a condolence call did they resume dating and marry soon afterward. Nothing precipitous about *their* decision and from that perspective, my parents could only consider my announcement that I would marry a man six months to the day after I had met him as impulsive, fraught with risk, and probably doomed to fail.

What was my rush to marry all about? For one thing, my boyfriend and I had already begun to live together and while that arrangement was not unheard of in the early sixties, it was decidedly unconventional. Worse (much worse), it was an implicit acknowledgment of premarital sex, which in my parent's lexicon bordered on sin. I had found that out the summer before I went off to college when a dark, brooding silence suddenly blanketed the relaxed vacation climate in our household following my parents' discovery that my sister had had sex with her boyfriend of several years. Already clued in by my sister and desperate to break the silence (in those days unable to tolerate any kind of conflict), I "innocently" asked my mother what was going on—to be told that she didn't want to tell me because she didn't want to "contaminate" me.

So I definitely was not imagining my parents' disapproval of my living with a man in an unmarried state even though I had been on my own for a number of years. Never mind that they knew and we knew that they knew while all of us maintained the fiction that none of us knew. (Several months after I was married, in a rare instance of humor that I cherish, my mother handed me a framed New Yorker cartoon showing two women talking over cocktails, one saying to the other, "I know that they know and we know that they know but we all act as if none of us knows.")

(It didn't take long for my parents to appreciate and admire my husband, however different he initially seemed. Toward the end of an awkward dinner the same evening I told them we were planning to marry, my father semi-complained to my mother that she hadn't yet had the light fixed in the standing globe just outside his study, whereupon my husband-to-be, familiar with basic electrical work and plumbing from his variety of earlier jobs, volunteered to fix it—and did so then and there.)

Another incentive to marrying quickly was my anxiety that the relationship was too good to be true, that it might vanish just as magically as the handsome blond man had appeared. Perhaps the legitimacy of marriage would make things solid enough to counter my doubts that one of us might find some deep flaw in the other and break it off. (Probably he, I thought, would leave me.) Knowing also how prone I was to denial and rationalization, I was afraid that I might have misconstrued the good stuff and would eventually find myself hurtling toward disaster instead of bliss.

My worry was exacerbated considerably by the fact that we met in August when Dr. L, my analyst at the time, was away.* By then I

---

*Thursday August 20th to be exact which I tend to consider our real anniversary; I still delight in the sequential symmetry as in, met on a Thursday, refound on a Friday and married on a Saturday, a kind of magical thinking for sure.

was sophisticated enough about the summer break to know that I might well have unconsciously acted out my need for her by finding a substitute. After all, I had always experienced interruptions in treatment, even weekends, as painful separations and waited restlessly for her return (a function of the transference yet again), reflecting my inability to control the comings and goings of an important person in my life.

I am hardly the only analysand to react to the disruptions of her analyst's vacation although the particulars will vary depending on dyad and the dynamics currently in play. For me the experience was usually about missing my analyst; for others it can range from welcome relief (about not having to pay) to some elaborate enactment that will take center stage, like that of the relatively new patient of mine, Samantha, who uprooted herself one August from the New Jersey home where she and her husband had been living for several years and "ended up" with an apartment about five blocks from my office. On my return in September, when I wondered to her about the geography of her move, she insisted they had been looking for some time and just "happened" to find a place nearby. The daughter of an unreliable, unpredictable alcoholic, it took years before Samantha could explore the elements of her growing attachment to and wish to be like me, her anger at me for abandoning her for my vacation and her desire to keep me under her watchful eye.

But getting back to my concern about the consequences of Dr. L's return to my new relationship, that September for the first time, I actually dreaded it and her power to ask a question that would press me to consider something I might have pushed to some un-thinkable corner of my mind. (At their best, analysts can do that with a timing and tact that makes it bearable to tolerate exploring some hidden corner of the mind.) But the challenge never came and by late fall I breathed a sigh of relief that my relationship had weathered Dr. L's analytic scrutiny and my boyfriend and I proceeded to marry, as I've said, six months to the day after we met. Today, recogniz-ing how much authority I had vested in Dr. L, I realize that I con-strued the absence of a devastating question from her as permission to proceed; it was permission I couldn't get from my parents and couldn't fully give to myself. Transference can work like that too.

As for my concern that I would be giving up one love (tennis) for another—came the first balmy spring weekend about six weeks into our marriage, my new husband and I went through our already typical back-and-forth-deferring to one another about what we wanted to do, and of course, the tennis courts were beckoning me. So what if he didn't know how to play? If he was willing to learn, I could certainly teach him. And that was the beginning of a tennis partnership that now seems inevitable if unforeseeable in kind or degree, although my husband still insists that I wrote it into our marriage contract in invisible ink.

Never in my wildest longings, which our relationship fulfilled beyond anything I hoped or imagined, had I considered the pos-sibility that when I stepped on a court to play my tennis of the day I would be facing my best friend across the net. Or that I would be married to a man who not only became my tennis partner but also quickly grew into a powerful and skilled competitor. More focused on the likely renunciation of the game for the relationship, I certainly did not anticipate that hours of playing handball and stickball on the streets of Brooklyn would have endowed this natural athlete to whom I was married with an inheritance of agility and street smarts: he may not have known the strokes or scoring of tennis but he brought to the game a whole new dimension of play for me.

But that's not all. As soon as he was holding his own, my husband became bored with endless rallies and suggested we ought to begin playing sets: what was the point of a game, he asked quite casually, if not to play it out to the end? What he said made sense, and since most of the things we had undertaken together so far had worked out well (understatement), I ignored my own history and accommodated to his suggestion with scarcely any hesitation. So almost as readily as we had eased into one another's lives, tennis eased its way into our joint one and became something we would continue to share in spring and summer, and on vacations too.

That was the very up-side. But what I didn't know in those halcyon early days was the huge psychological down-side that lay ahead. Suffice it to say, playing sets gradually pushed me out of the sanctuary* of rallies into the heat of the game and forced me to compete. At first I won easily, relaxed about my edge of skills; then we settled into the period during which I felt most comfortable, of splitting sets, an extended middle phase throughout which we seemed to have arrived at a balance of power, an equality between peers. (In a crunch I could still play to my husband's weaknesses, confident that he would

---

*Courtesy of the late Alison Danzig, sports writer for the New York Times, who coined the exquisitely economic phrase, "the sanctity of deuce." Any tennis player will know what I mean.

be hard pressed to come up with a shot I couldn't handle.)

It wasn't long however, before he could return a winning shot from me with a challenging shot of his own—backhand, cross court, or wicked forehand. (I say *wicked*, half out of admiration for the magnificence of the forehand my husband can make at will from the backhand corner, seemingly out of position, looking for all the world as if he has mis-hit the ball; depending on my mood and other variables, the remaining half comes from pique over a shot that doesn't look classic and is sneaky.) Naturally my husband delights in it since he's not burdened with the prohibitions I have had to strip away layer by layer as I have tried to deal with the relationship between my father and myself. But backhand or forehand, sneaky or not, I soon learned that I'd better start running to retrieve whatever good shot I may have sent my husband's way, an escalation of my game in reaction to his, which he learned in response to me and my love of the game.

It is nothing short of remarkable to me just how much our games, individually and together, have grown and improved over time in an ongoing dialectic of advances and fun, particularly in light of the paucity of our exposure to other players. Indeed, had we in some other lifetime gone our separate ways, I am certain each of us might have reached a higher level of play. I'll even confess to a sometime worry that my husband, had he been inclined, might have been even a stronger player, able to overpower me and take more, if not most, of the sets we play.

Apparently he's had the same idea (or is it fantasy?). Quite a number of years ago, when the subject of tennis came up over dinner with new friends, one of them (the man of course) asked which of us was the better player (meaning who beat whom). With due modesty, I answered that my husband and I were equal enough to split sets, to which my husband remarked that I was a superb player who had taught him how to play. Then, shifting from conversational to teasing mode, he added that if he put his mind to it I'd never be able to take another set from him. Off-court warfare to be sure, but in the orbit of my insecurities, it immediately entered the repertoire of my undoing, on a bad day at any rate, when I worryingly remind myself that many a truth is spoken in jest.

At its best, ours is a game characterized by sets that can stretch to 10-all (we tend to eschew the tiebreaker) and by long, steady rallies punctuated by magnificent duels under the hot sun, attacks of parry and riposte (usually initiated by my husband), accompanied by occasional banter or other forms of psychic warfare designed to throw me off (also usually initiated by my husband, master of the gentle tease). But for years the best could turn to worst when a drop shot or blistering cross court from my husband could rudely interrupt the glorious reverie of a rally, morphing him into an aggressive opponent who had not followed the rules as they were originally engraved in my head, instantly undoing the internal balance that mostly allowed me to enjoy the game in those early years.

I also still continue to wonder if my husband was counting on my tendency to self-destruct when he challenged me to a tennis match to resolve the greatest conflict of our married life—whether or not to have the third child I kept pushing for against his practical arguments that we already had a girl and a boy in whom we delighted, we lived in the most expensive city in the world and we were financially squeezed. Why not be content with how much we already had? But every time I passed a carriage with an infant or toddler, my desire was fueled and I simply could not let the matter rest. Until one day, as we were about to play our morning round of tennis, my husband threw down the gauntlet, "Take me 6-0 and we'll have another child." And so I did, proof of the stubbornness of which I am capable when desire or passion are riding high.

The spirit of full disclosure, however, warrants an addendum. A few months earlier, Debbie, a seven-year-old playmate of our daughter Elizabeth had been stricken with encephalitis and died: one day she was part of an essential threesome in the country, another day she was gone. Sometime after our challenge match when I asked my husband what had really won him over to agree to have another child, he replied, "Debbie's death," leaving me to ponder forever if he had already come to the decision independently and was enough in control of his game to lose to me love-6. It's a power I sometimes give him still, on a bad day, at any rate.

Clearly, my husband is a relaxed, laid-back person who instinctively seems to calibrate the precise amount of energy required for a particular task; not surprisingly, he plays tennis in a similarly low key. In fact, my father who judged everything through his prism of hard work, used to comment only half-jokingly that my husband looked lazy on the court. But what my father mistook for laziness was a diffident mix of ease and comfort, a deceptive cover for power and control that to this day can catch me off guard.

I, on the other hand, am generally restless and filled with energy bursting to be released, prone to sudden crescendos and shifts; I throw myself into the game as if each point were the most crucial, a definite residue of doing my father-mandated best. Still, although tennis can take me over at times, it has never been more than a part of our family whole, which, in obvious counterpoint to how I grew up, has been shaped by juggling the changing variety of all our interests and needs. (While the children all play, perhaps it is not surprising that none has taken to tennis with the ferocity that has been mine; moreover, to give Josh his due, when he took his first set from me, tennis was just one of a number of his sports, football and basketball being primary at the time.)

Nevertheless, tennis definitely is identified with my husband and me, so much so, that people who have witnessed our passion for the game during the summer are incredulous to learn that we abandon it in winter. Mostly we're too busy but also by late fall we're surfeited, my husband with the single-minded monster I can become, I with myself and the intensity of it all. Besides, hibernation is not a bad thing even if it does mean I need longer each spring to get into a groove again, thus feeding my annual despair that I have lost the rhythm and my touch. And that too is one more over-reaction of my tennis self that my husband tolerates with amusement and equanimity.

But then he has a much more settled sense of self than I—and therein lies the rub for me. Off-court this characteristic has mostly fueled our marriage in positive ways (he slows me down while I speed him up), but on-court, faced with the very same pressures that can undo me, my husband is able to maintain his equanimity. Indeed, it is his strong suit, and when all is said and done, it is in *that* difference between us that the crux of the tennis matter resides—the necessity for me to maintain balance and parity between us at all times, not to be the same as but to be equal in most respects.

This is an ideal, an inversion really, of the glaring inequalities lodged in the formative models of my youth—the relationships between parent and child, work and play, mother and father, and by extension, between women and men. All of these imbalances I brought with me to the marriage and spent much of my life trying to deny, to circumvent, or to repair. It is the paradigm that lies at the heart of the game I play and, more importantly, at the psychological center of myself. Yet it is a theme that my early analyses left relatively untouched.

Penis envy? I dealt with that the first times around, I told Dr. Stevenson blithely in my preliminary consultation with him (I blush to recall). Actually, that was true, as far as it went. But what I hadn't dealt with was penis awe—awe that is, of the power of men inherited through my father to intimidate me and hold me in thrall. What else was it when my husband took charge with a blistering shot or captured my match from my commanding lead? What else but a show of power that reminded me all too well of what he had and I lacked? What else was it that evoked feelings I hadn't dealt with in my first treatments, among them, the sometimes toxic envy that awaited me when I stepped on the court (breeding ground for reminders of differences or weaknesses) and my tenacious denial or suppression of anger in almost all conscious respects. For all the gains I'd made on the couches of Drs. R and L, the significance of tennis as a unifying metaphor in my psychic life had been quite overlooked.

Several years after terminating with Dr. L, I returned to touch base, to fill her in on how positively my life seemed to be moving along. Attributing much of the positive momentum to psychoanalysis whose potentiating power had freed me to go beyond the constricted realm of my mother's life with my father, I continued in lighter (but no less serious) vein, "even my tennis game has improved." To which she humorlessly replied, "Psychoanalysis is a rather expensive way to improve it, don't you think?"

I can still feel the disquieting annoyance stirred by Dr. L's seeming disregard of the importance of tennis to me, annoyance that I characteristically quashed at the time with the rationalization that she, still object of my gratitude and veneration, was just off. I certainly did not challenge her about that, any more than I ever did about anything during my work with her, most especially the matter of differences and my suppression of anger, let alone rage or hate. Of course, I wasn't aware of them then, but apparently neither was she.

And of course, tennis was the last thing on my mind when I began therapy with Dr. Stevenson, certain that my difficulties lay in the arena of my professional life. But if the extent to which tennis was to work its way into the treatment came as a surprise, its evolution as part of the shared vocabulary of our work was astonishing. Still more so was the eventual discovery, especially plunged as I was into the intense endeavor that had me mostly weeping for the first several years, that our work would ultimately free me to play, starting on the playing field created by the analyst, the analysand and the couch.

There was, for example, the time early on when I described a mistake I'd made with a patient (probably an interpretation I'd missed or something I'd said that might better have been left unsaid) and I was struggling with the familiar mortification and shame engendered by yet more evidence of my being less than perfectly competent or legitimate in relation to my work—heightened of course by the transference to Dr. Stevenson as the over-idealized father without flaw. Breaking into the bleak silence that followed my now regular storm of weeping, Dr. Stevenson wondered aloud whether I might consider trying to serve again, a second serve to my patient.

It was, I believe, his way of soothing my anguish with gentle humor, of softening my shame. But his gently teasing question also offered another perspective—perhaps I might try to accept some of the imperfections that come with being human—at the same time that it implicitly encouraged me to try again. If my first serve missed, might I allow myself the luxury of a second, one not about failure but about an alternative? When is it not helpful to have a variety of shots in one's arsenal? Indeed, wasn't my historic refusal even to learn a second serve, an irrational insistence on perfection the first time around and a lingering identification with my father? And wasn't that embedded in my resistance to change, in my clinging to the outmoded ideals that set off my cycles of hopelessness, anger, loss of control and shame?

An even more provocative question had caught me off guard on an earlier occasion. I had begun a session complaining about the weekend in which, true to form, I had blown away a significant lead in a set with my husband. Still sitting up, I half-expected to see an empathic nod from Dr. Stevenson, so I was floored when he neutrally asked me whether I had considered the possibility that my husband might be the better player of us two.

A drop shot from my analyst? So early in the game? In those days, quite incapable of laughing either at myself or with him, I definitely felt put out by its spin although in that session I wasn't able to admit how annoyed I was. I'm still not sure whether he was teasing, checking out my reality-testing, the extent of denial and grandiosity to which I might be prone, or all or none of the above—but by the time I recovered enough from what felt like an aggressive shot to respond in the next session, I said that allowing for the variables of weather, mood, strokes or style and for the differences in our genders and respective strengths, I believed that my husband and I were close to even—not the same but equal enough to balance out.

What I didn't know then was that exploring the ramifications of Dr. Stevenson's question and my androgynous ideal of being different from but equal to a man (not the same but no less competent and effective) would be at the heart of the analysis. Or that my need to maintain balance between partners was the historical root of, and organizing ideal behind, my desire to reach and sustain a state of grace as a powerful woman who could hold her own in competition with a man, on or off the court.

But that androgynous ideal and the imperative driving it were not based on a mature compromise that reflected coming to terms with what I could not have or be. Rather, they were fashioned on a primitive model that denied that differences existed or insisted that they could always be evened out if they did. Underneath this model lay a universe of fantasies spawned in a primary process world (limitless in time and space, not conditioned by narrative logic), in which I could be both masculine and feminine with no conflict of interest or missing parts, safe from confrontations with reality that remind one that there are limits to having or being all. (And "one" is the correct pronoun, since regardless of gender, in our fantasies we are capable of being both.)

The opportunities and challenges for finding or losing balance over the course of development are, of course, a part of the human condition. For me, the functional corollary to the theme of balance was to make whatever adjustments would maintain it; hence my need to level or minimize if not obliterate differences whenever found. For much of my life, I had been locked into a detection system that searched out differences and registered fractions of degrees. That process, almost totally without shading, subtlety, modulation or humor to temper the extremes, would often connote something negative or lesser about me in relation to others and it was that which had the power to throw me off balance, far out of proportion to the matter at hand. These workings of my internal drama found fertile ground on the tennis court and from that perspective, tennis was not the exception but the rule, least of all a game in the best sense of the word but rather a psychic playing field replete with temptations to enact, wrestle, cope with, or deny the profound and exquisite challenge of coming to terms with the difference(s) between the sexes.

We are all governed by that theme, its individual variations weaving their major or minor, contrapuntal or melodic strands through our lives. Even its denial is a variation on the theme. For me, the theme had been dominant except when the experience of maternity provided a respite, for it was as a mother that I began to be my own person, to feel powerful in my own right. Fulfilled by the reciprocity of needs and satisfactions between me and my children, I felt valuable to others and therefore to myself.

But children grow, and as mine needed me less in the active care-taking sense, as they stretched beyond the orbit in which I was oh-so-transiently the center of their universe, I was pulled back into the conflicted realm of the past. Even the emerging professional identity that had evolved from the very part-time therapeutic tutoring I had undertaken soon after our first child was born could not relieve the feelings of depletion that crept into the increasing distance between my children and me. My child-self had been quiescent while the adult had gone about the business of life, but now, in my fifties, I was caught in a vortex of loss and soon found myself immersed in struggles from which I had naively thought myself removed. Undoubtedly, this burgeoning sense of crisis was exacerbated by my father's increasing frailty and imminent death. Intellectually I had always known that he would die, but I could not really believe it; had he not always been able to control matter with mind?

It was also around this time that I found myself becoming increasingly vulnerable to life events, themselves more and more often filtered through the internal prism that confirmed the inadequate self I had been all along. The good-enough sense of self that had evolved with maternity seemed to be vanishing in inverse proportion to the actual accomplishments of my life: these felt insubstantial, even cosmetic, while my mistakes felt true and real. It was this self that began to intrude in my professional life and to erupt on the tennis court with a frequency and intensity impossible to deny (as evidenced by the black moods and explosions of swearing that would overtake me when I played poorly or lost).

Now it seems obvious to me what it was about me and my game that could make me lose at my critical moments while my husband could win at his. Fully at home with his strengths and weaknesses, unlike me, my husband did not confuse the loss of a set with loss of self-worth; when he competed, it was not primarily about a need to prove his worth, to himself or to anyone else. So a formidable backhand that would fail to clear the net, a beautiful drive just a fraction out, even a sloppy shot that could cost him a game or set, were simply bad luck or errors he could ignore and go on to the next point. (And on a good day, so it was for me.) But while my husband was playing a game, I was playing with a vulnerable self, a state of being from which it doesn't take much to lose one's balance—and mine was precarious, whether about work or play, competence or vulnerability, male or female, in reality, or in psychic time and space.

On a bad day, when my psychic realities overpowered the more objective ones of my game, my errors became proof of my inadequacy and I became my own worst enemy. Then, instead of my playing the game, the game played me. To make matters worse, once caught up in the mind-set of inadequacy, I unconsciously envied (and hated) my husband's ability to remain calm and contained. Envy is a nasty crime of the mind for which I had to punish myself by losing when I could have won (the punishment to fit the crime.) And worse. Once my failed sense of self kicked in (the demon at my core), however slight the trigger or the injury, the verdict seemed final and beyond repair, the glass half-empty instead of half-full.

In the profession, such errors or slights to an imperfect, unlovable self are called narcissistic injuries. And they are. However trivial or insignificant in reality, they go to the very center of one's being and radiate out with a searing sense of shame, sometimes pain, and almost always humiliation. To someone who is struggling with a vulnerable self, the least reminder can be a wound or even an earthquake with tremors and aftershocks of varying intensity. And I was just such a someone.

For all the tools I had acquired in my early analyses, it was this about me that accounted for the psychological edge my husband had over me in tennis that I couldn't grasp. If, in the context of a fragile sense of self and self-esteem (like mine), one is thrown off one's balance and also lacks the tools to *self-regulate* (as I did), to comfort and reassure (mother oneself) or simply shrug knowing an episode will pass—one feels incapable and unlovable, alone in the universe. And since there will always be someone or something to upset a fragile internal scale, such a vulnerability can be a toxin to joy and delight until it is uncovered and worked through (need I add here?) as in a psychoanalysis. Small wonder that my capacity to hold on to a good-enough sense of self was so tenuous, a goal about which I was clueless at first and toward which I would have to inch my way with Dr. Stevenson.

So I am unmasked. What I have been describing, this extreme sensitivity to slight changes, to subtle shifts in the heat and cold of the emotional universe, and the even greater difficulty regulating the internal thermostat once the balance has been upset—all this exposed on the court—had nothing to do with tennis and everything to do with a narcissistically vulnerable self. Call it what one will, sensitivity, attribute, peculiarity or temperamental state, this fragile narcissism is part of a constellation and what people ordinarily mean when they talk about poor self-esteem. (When they do so in my office, I inwardly sigh in empathic contemplation of the depths to which they might have to plunge in order to bring about some repair.)

As with resistance, despite the term's pejorative connotations, narcissism is not in and of itself a negative thing. On the contrary, a positive primary narcissism is a prerequisite for a healthy sense of self and self-esteem. (And here, counter to what many erroneously construe as the excessive self-admiration of Narcissus, I would argue that a positive sense of self is what he lacked and pined for, looking for sustenance and reassurance from the calm reflection of the pool to counter a depleted, critical self within.)

To complicate the constellation, some narcissistic personalities are driven to inflate themselves in compensatory ways: in them grandiosity and self-importance noticeably prevail; it is they who can abruptly, often cruelly, discard someone who has been most close, usually because the other has failed to flatter or sufficiently feed their self-esteem. Indeed, they can be hard to take as they struggle with denial in their way, trying to conceal from themselves and everyone else the flawed, worthless selves within.

For people who fall as I did into the depleted group with a flaw at the self's core, emptiness may be masked by wretchedness or humility accompanied by a relentless drive to achieve. Those who suffer from this kind of affliction will undoubtedly identify with the controlling and painful aspects of the disease: nothing is ever good enough and even states of grace are transient, while mistakes or bruises feel like the most real and negative thing. As Jason, a patient of mine talking in contemplative mode in session about his golf game, mused: "Why is it that when one plays one's best game, it is only an accident of that particular game, but when one plays badly, that's what one's game is really about?"

By that time, I already knew quite a bit about Jason's fragile self-esteem. The youngest of six children, he had grown up believing that he was the cause of his mother's sometimes suicidal depression and despair. Son also of an authoritarian man, Jason was himself an extremely controlled person, convinced that he had been a drain from the moment of his birth; he juggled depression and profound sadness with internal howls of rage beneath his rigid efforts to keep himself reined in. Golf was one of the few arenas where his passion could be expressed although frequently his frustrations erupted into rage.

On the personal front, his relations were unconsciously constricted by his refusal to get close to anyone lest he become a "despised nuisance" again. Jason had married a very dependent woman like his mother and soon found the relationship intolerable and after a year he abruptly ended it, the leaving itself an expression of aggression and revenge. This constriction was expressed in the transference as anxiety about becoming too close to me. Jason's corresponding wish to damage me by leaving the treatment buttressed his fear of staying and becoming the rejected "nuisance" to me that he had been to his mother: from the perspective of his internal world, the latter eventuality was an outcome to be avoided at all costs

"Never again," one often says to oneself unconsciously about some psychic injury or trauma from the past. And indeed Jason ultimately could tolerate being only so close. Despite my interpretive efforts and the relief he had begun to feel, especially as he came to understand what had happened between him and his wife, he told me at the end of a session without warning that he had decided to discontinue therapy (just the way he had separated from his wife). He did continue a while longer but then stopped, using the pressures of work as a 'reason' although until then, he had managed to juggle things well enough. ("Reality is the best resistance," one of my supervisors once said to me, and oh 'tis true, 'tis true.)

Jason's decision to stop treatment was partially influenced by his insurance company which ceased reimbursing for his sessions with me after a year and a half. As the claims adjuster said in a telephone follow-up to my protest, since Jason was no longer in the crisis that had brought him to treatment, since he was not suicidal (never had been) or severely depressed (never had been), he was not sick enough to treat: "He's one of the walking wounded but we don't reimburse for that."

I have no doubt that Jason's reimbursement would have continued had he been on medication, path of least resistance and far and away the "preferred" mode of psychological treatment from the perspective of insurance companies. Of course, it's not only the insurance companies who focus on symptom relief and short term care but also many physicians themselves who push pharmaceuticals, medicating many who might suffer from psychic pain, deficits in maintaining connections with others in a sustained or intimate way, compulsions to achieve because nothing is ever enough—people who are often highly functional but not "sick" enough to treat. But nowhere is the rush to label and treat more egregious than when it comes to the use and abuse of drugs as the primary treatment instead of "in conjunction with" or "in addition to" psychotherapy.

Among too numerous examples, I am reminded of Mrs. J who came to me for consultation saying that she was a "depressive" and needed to remain on drugs: she had been on them ever since her diagnosis for postpartum depression over thirty years before and had regularly seen a psychiatrist once a week. After all the years of her very expensive once-a-week treatment, she seemed not at all to understand how to go about dealing with conflicts in her life, relying instead on pills to mute her anxiety whenever a conflictual situation came up, with her husband, other family members, or at work. That is, she felt hopeless about her capacity to change or to cope.

At first expecting the same "maintenance" from me as she had gotten from the psychiatrist whom she could no longer afford, Mrs. J was angry when I questioned her diagnostic labeling of herself. Then, a conflict came up with one of her children and when I wondered why she had remained silent and not even tried to work it out with him, her associations went back to her sense of hopelessness about change and the alcoholic mother who sent her to boarding schools starting when she was six and had neglected and disappointed her over and again. Vulnerable and confused, Mrs. J had never questioned her mother about anything and she had suffered in silence and confusion lest she lose what little she had; over time her defenses had become characterological for her. And while it would be unreasonable to attribute all to Mrs. J's being locked into a definition of herself as a "depressive" who needed medication to cope, it certainly contributed to her sense of helplessness about being able to act or to change, a primary theme of our work.

But back to matters of primary narcissism and some of the pertinent personal elements therein, that is, the matter of my mother and me. For really, after all I've said about the complexities of development, how could my struggles be only about my father? Like invisible ink that requires a solution to bring the figures into relief, the mother of my childhood needed the light of hindsight and the lens of psychoanalysis to emerge—for her essential emotional absence in my life was the inverse of the father who was too much. Even the specialness that adhered to her, in retrospect, derived primarily from the magic of her connection to him.

By all appearances, my mother was the enviable kind: she was beautiful (I thought the most beautiful in the world), likeable and charming, so much so, that every year I couldn't wait for Open School Week, not because I wanted to know what my teachers thought of me but because I was excited to show her off.

I was proud of how she looked in the Red Cross uniform she wore driving ambulances to meet WWII servicemen returning home, enchanted by her reports of the crushes they developed on her (much to her delight), impressed by her cheerful efficiency when she was in charge of coordinating New York City's volunteers for

Stevenson's presidential campaign, and thrilled by her able introduction of Eleanor Roosevelt in connection with her role as fund
raiser for concerts sponsored by the Lower East Side Neighborhood
Association (LENA).

My mother ran the household with a smooth efficiency that
my father praised, calling her "practical Lil," an extension, he often reminded us and her, of the best secretary he ever had. But
that was a testament of her service to him and to us, not to any
achievements of her own. In truth, my father's overvaluation of
work (of his kind of real work) put my mother's role of service in
sorry relief, compromising my positive identification with her as I
grew up and magnifying my sense of futility about ever managing to
measure up.

Even her particular spheres of competence diminished by the
time my sister and I were married with children of our own and
she became unable (or unwilling) to sustain whatever activities she
might start, often claiming some illness (mostly minor) as the reason
she could not continue. It was clear to us all that a pattern had set in.
By that time she had also begun to complain openly about the con-
strictions of her life with my father and to assert her resentment by
drinking as she waited for him to come home from work. (That was
a behavior my father could not penetrate with reason although surely
he tried, and being reasonable, tried again, to no avail; this was not
only confusing, but painful to him.) Be that as it may, it would take
me many years to reconfigure my internal equation of woman/wife
with my mother, confounded as it was by my father's manifest message that meaningful work is what mattered, gender did not.

Thus when I told him as a little girl that I wanted to be a nurse and mother when I grew up (the two being then conflated in my mind), without missing a beat he recommended that I consider becoming a doctor instead. Excited by the suggestion (which I mistook for attunement with me), I immediately adopted it, unknowingly abandoning parts of myself that would have differentiated me from him, like an early identification with my mother witnessed by my intense play with dolls (especially bathing and comforting them as if they were real, in the process also trying to mother myself). Retaining some vestiges of my original plan, however, I did decide to become a pediatrician and take care of children in that way (an unconscious compromise, I can't resist pointing out).

When I eventually did become a doctor, it was not the M.D. kind. A few years after I had completed my Ph.D. (which my father as a trustee of NYU publicly conferred on me as we hugged), I tried to share with him the sense of rightness, even inevitability, I felt about the professional direction of my life. He smiled but asked, "Are you sure?" meaning, didn't I wish that I had become the "real," as in the medical kind?

For years I remained hurt and angry at my father's resistance to learning much of anything about what I did, certainly more so than I was at my mother's continuing inability (until she died) to pronounce "psychoanalysis," the only word I ever heard her consistently stumble upon. Obviously, it was more important to me that my father understood. I knew that he was proud of me, but it was clear that he believed psychiatrists (M.D.s) knew more than psychologists (Ph.D.s), a misconception common to many who confuse surviving the rigors of medical school with therapeutic competence.

It's also possible that my father was intimidated by the sheer fact of my being a psychologist, as people often are. Countless are the jokes, including those of one friend who often greets me with her idea of a humorous query when she asks whether I've cured any "crazies" today. (I know that she is a believer in the power of therapy and includes herself as one of the "crazies," but still!) Or of those who, on learning what I do, talk about needing to lie down on my couch so I can read their minds. I certainly remember my own discomfort when speaking with a psychiatrist on the telephone, somehow fantasizing that he or she could know what was going on in my mind. Similarly, I sometimes have to remind myself that my benevolent recommendation during a consultation that someone undertake therapy or an analysis can be alien and terrifying to a person who knows nothing about the work. Misconceptions and fantasies abound. (And here, I'll admit that it drives me crazy that some therapists who have never undergone the rigors of analytic training call themselves analysts; usually what they practice is a version of therapy, not analysis, and that tends to give psychoanalysis a bad name.)

The key, in fact, is not in the degree but in the training that comes after it. For instance, budding psychiatrists have only minimal education in the theory of human development and their first practical exposure usually comes in a hospital where the most extreme cases of mental illness are found and medication is the first choice of treatment taught. In marked contrast, Ph.D. or Psy.D. candidates in psychology study development, theories of personality, and different approaches to therapy and testing; to fulfill the requirements for the degree they must accumulate many hours of supervised clinical experience in diagnosis and treatment, implement research and write a dissertation as well.

And in the case of those who go on to become psychoanalysts, that's even not all. Depending on the particular institute, candidates (as they are called) study theory and clinical practice, conduct two supervised or control analyses (three or four times a week) for a minimum of two to three years and undergo a psychoanalysis of their own (training analysis). Unlike the very early days under Freud when an analysis sometimes lasted even less than a year, a contemporary training analysis usually lasts a minimum of four to five years and beyond.

(In 2005, New York, as has several other states, passed a law granting a license in psychoanalysis to those who have undergone "psychoanalytic" training but who might not otherwise be licensed as a mental health professional (Ph.D's, M.D.'s, or C.S.W.'s). While this might seem a positive step, it's quite controversial since the state's standard for psychoanalytic training is minimal, when compared to the rigorous requirements associated with the classical institutes described above. To display the license of a psychoananlyst in the absence of those rigors—a long-term analysis, a number of extensively supervised control cases of 3 or 4 times a week—certainly has the potential to mislead a potential analysand.)

Which brings me back to Dr. Stevenson—to whom I said when we met in consultation that I was there to talk about the pattern of mistakes I seemed to keep making in my work and my difficulty in dealing with anger (that of my patients and my own). Then there was the related question of why I seemed to be so restless and unable to sit still, like my father, or why I seemed to be more and more driven by my work. Secure in the belief that my earlier treatments had opened up a path different from that of my mother's life with my father, I was quite clueless about the formative influence of my mother's emotional unavailability as a source of comfort and self-esteem, or the degree to which that absence might be contributing to some inchoate sense that I was not fully living in my own skin, that I was "missing out" on the intensity of things.

If an analysis has a theme, and I believe that each one does, I would say that my first analyses facilitated a good-enough separation from the kingdom of my father and the conflicts he bequeathed; they also enabled me to become sufficiently at home with myself as a woman to throw myself into maternity and domesticity in distinguishing and healthy ways. (Though l was still under the illusion that competition with women was irrelevant to me, I was in fact quite competitive with my mother as a mother in my own right, proud to be more competent, more active, and more effective than she in the multiple roles I could and did fill.)

But only in my analysis with Dr. Stevenson did I come to apprehend the importance of the primary dyad, the relationship between mother and child, and to recognize the omissions that robbed me of the kinds of interactions that can shape a confident sense of self, that left me feeling empty and bereft, and conditioned me to wait. That also explained the mysterious "homesick" feeling I used to get for my mother (even into my teen years), which I certainly didn't understand since she was there. Or so I thought.

Although Freud certainly recognized the crucial importance of the mother as the first "object" for a child, he focused on the oedipal conflict whose dynamics by definition involve mother and father and child. It was those who came after him (Winnicott, Klein, Bowlby, the Attachment theorists of today) who turned their attention to the impact of our earliest (pre-oedipal) experiences on our capacity to internalize a sense of being taken care of if we need soothing, nurtured if we need feeding, contained if we are tired or angry. It was the absence of such positive experiences that characterized my relationship with my mother, clearly an omission not consciously identified until mid-life, but ingrained nonetheless in my earliest versions of myself. Moreover, it was those very early experiences that constituted my psychic universe and organized my life.

So it was not only about my father; it was also very much about my mother or rather, the emotional absence of her. And filling that void, if an essential truth be known, has been a huge part of why my husband has been such a good partner for me. Not only was he different from my father, even more important, my low-keyed tolerant husband listened to me, he paid attention to me, he made me feel cared for at the same time as I was caring for the children and him, and in so doing—he gave me the gift of some of the mothering of which I had been bereft. On the tennis court, his generous way of competing created space for me to feel safe, and in the process, nurtured too. That very same mothering gift may also help explain the magnitude of my sense of betrayal when he played an aggressive game against me. After all, "a mother has to be there to be left,"* and, lacking as I did, the capacity to mother myself, it gave my husband enormous power in my life.

---

*Taken from the title of an article by Erna Furman which begins with that quote by Anna Freud who recognized the crucial importance of the mother's availability, in order for the child to move away—and come back.

When I look back at my earliest years with my mother through the lens of reconstruction and transference, clearly my reactions to waiting did not originate with my father, on the court or off. And what stands out now in bold relief is the degree to which the passive experiences of waiting, watching or wanting shaped my overall sense of insignificance and laid the groundwork for my experiences with my father to take hold. Beyond that, they all instilled in me a persistent pressure to prove myself, thereby forging my driving urgency to be at the center of things, to matter, to be in control, never the person on the outside, whether at work, at play or in love.

For one psychological thing, too much waiting grounded me in an economy of restlessness and pain instead of in the pleasure and satisfaction our early shared experiences can and should bring about. On some subterranean level, it also left me terrified of rage and aggression, my own and others', since I rarely was immersed in the exquisite security of containment and well-being that a mother's devoted and responsive ministrations can engender over developmental time. The absence of such soothing and affectionate ties of maternal love that form our boundaries and dawning awareness of ourselves and another, perhaps clarifies what undoubtedly propelled me even more in the direction of my father instead.

The molecular configuration around and about waiting began at my birth and immediately had to do with delay and tension where fullness and contentment should have been instead. Waiting to be fed, to be held, and for someone to pay attention, were among my earliest experiences, formative and profound. Each individually might have seemed an unfortunate condition to which a child had to learn to adapt, and I for the most certainly did, perhaps too well. Cumulatively, however, they thwarted the development of a healthy sense of self and in time became characterological and diminishing, enough to transcend realities of time or place or even satisfaction (as illustrated by my joy at hitting the few balls my father pitched to me on those spring mornings in the Bronx).

I'm not talking about the inevitable lapses of attunement that occur between even the best of mothers and her child but about a pattern of omissions and postponement that thwarted the development of a sense of safety and trust whereby I could feel that my needs would be reliably and comfortably met. It is just the devoted, ministering behaviors of a good-enough mothering person, repeated over increments of time and developmental space, that become the bedrock determinants of the way we feel and act, defining where a benevolent sense of self and other begins and ends. How else, if not from our earliest examples, do we learn to mother ourselves?

Obviously, I've learned a lot about these matters over the years, perhaps most as a mother to children of my own, for what I know of my early history derives not from conscious memory but from myriad revisionist renderings, starting with my mother's explanation that she had followed the dictates of the child-rearing authorities of the day: these decreed that an infant must wait for four hours between feedings, no matter how long or hard she cried. (Her incapacity to go with anything new or different, Dr. Spock for one example, would have precluded my mother's seeking advice from any but established authorities of the day.)

Surely such rigidity toward an infant, much of whose crying signaled hunger, was misplaced. But my mother, the daughter of an authoritarian man (said to have slapped her when she returned from a prom twenty minutes past the midnight curfew he had imposed), was remarkably out of touch with her feelings and either must not have been aware of any contradictory impulses or could not act on them if she was. But in the familial chain through which my mother passed her respect for authority on to me, the absence of nurturing and attunement left me likewise out of touch with, even indifferent to, my needs (bodily and other).

Trying to soften the cruelty of her tale of the hours I had to wait to be fed, in later years my mother claimed that she ended up crying too, apparently compelled to suffer along with me rather than relieve us both if it meant she had to break a rule. And that is a clue to my nutty insistence on playing tennis into almost my ninth month of pregnancy or my compulsion to play when feeling ill, that is, my ignorance of the physical manifestations of the denial of my own needs. Many of these surfaced with Dr. Stevenson in the form of stomach aches and sudden cramps as the analysis became the forum for those memories to emerge.

I realize how revealing this is about my mother. However, I write without intent to blame and with real sadness about how much we both missed, just as I mourn the emptiness of my memory traces of the beautiful mother and the cooler sins of omissions. It was my aunt who brought treats for us when she returned home from work, my aunt or my sister to whom I usually went for comfort when I was upset, and it was why, underneath the excitement of my aunt's marriage rather late in her life when I was thirteen, I felt a surge of sadness and loss that I didn't comprehend. For other than my aunt or my sister, there was only Jenny, the old-fashioned Italian greengrocer who fondly indulged me.

A bittersweet memory: it was in Jenny's small kingdom that I discovered my taste for green peas fresh from the pod, and Jenny who gave me the affectionate appellation, "the green-pea-girl." While my mother was deciding what she might take home that day, I would help myself to two or three pods from one of the colorful tiered baskets lining the floor, peeling the string that zipped the sides together, crunching the sweet orbs. Soon I wanted a few more but, worried that I might be scolded for my greed, tried to hold back. My appetite usually won out however, and just as my mother would interrupt my reach, Jenny would invite me to help myself to more, a bittersweet experience of both indulgence and greed.

And yet. The essentials of development are layered, testament to the unique intersection of constitution, heritage and environment that comprise an individual and his or her sense of self. Moreover, our earliest experiences occur in some primal internal time and space that is inchoate and without boundaries, the more so because we lack the words to articulate our images and sensations. Not until we acquire the tools of language, reason, and conscious memory, can we begin to organize and to make sense of our internal universe and to accommodate to that which comes from without.

None of the omissions was I aware of growing up. In fact, I became highly functional and proud of my capacity to take care of others, even complacent about my seeming absence of need. But the ancient past always leaves its imprint on the present. It textures my unrealistic impatience and anxiety in any situation that requires me to wait; it also explains my tendency to stretch time to the limits, a kind of one-upmanship that often ends with my magical hoping for the best, that a train will pull into the station just as I rush through the turnstile, that a taxi will appear the moment I step out to hail one, that traffic will not be heavy enough to make me wait.

The imprint of the past even shows in my only superficial compliance with rules I am always trying to subvert. For instance, much as I contend that it is important to begin and end an analytic hour on time and for the most part practice what I preach, I still cannot (or is it will not?) rid myself of the poor habit of arriving at my office, coffee cup in hand, just under the wire for my first session of the day. (Understandably this behavior sometimes stirs complaints from patients—one feeling neglected, another worried that I might be ill—who surely would rather see me waiting for them. Still, although my struggle about time obviously originates with me, what my patients experience or fantasize while waiting is about them and grist for their mill.)

After all, we are all ultimately insignificant in the scheme of things—except to those in our most immediate universe, and coming to terms with that is one of our most commonly shared existential themes. But not to have had some sense of value or importance at the center of another's world, not to have ever felt even the fleeting power to command what one wants or needs, not to have experienced the capacity to affect or enchant another in the potentiating and expanding days of infancy and toddlerhood—those are diminishing blows to a developing soul that can leave a crater of emptiness behind. In place of optimism or empowerment, doubt and insufficiency fill the vacuum and create an endless pressure that keeps one forever in pursuit, never quite able to savor achievements when they might be truly ours. Like winning a game from love-forty or, better yet, from forty-love.

epilogue

Let me tell you about people my age. The worst thing is others as-sume you have developed your character by now. The trouble with middle age is they think you are fully formed. (Caravaggio)

Michael Ondaetje, **The English Patient**

At the beginning of the summer following the one in which Josh took his first set from me, I played the first set of the season with our other son Seth. He was rusty, having not played since the previous summer and although I won, it was clear to me that the writing was on the wall. Later on that afternoon he played a set with his father whom he always challenges in a magnificent, oedipal way—a latter day incarnation (I can't resist adding) of the small boy, sweet-smelling from his evening bath, tackling his newly-arrived-from-work father to the bed in a free form wrestling match of hugs, challenges, yells and grunts, arm-locks and leg-grips, a duet with all the accouterments of his love for his father and his father's love for him.

Unlike the wrestling matches from which there never seemed to be a clear winner, Seth lost the set to his father. Still, the score of 4-6 was a definite indication of his potential to overtake us both. Earlier, while warming up, we had talked about his game and I had remarked that he had it all on his side: incredible power, stamina, and increasing age (which in his case was positive, bringing with it the experience of maturity and a brake on the impatience that tended to be the source of many of his mistakes). His father and I, on the other hand, were also getting older and that again was to his advantage. We might still have the groundstrokes and skill, but at some point soon (that summer, I thought), our games would slip back a little more and the balance that for so long had been in the ascendance for me would level out; with that, Seth would take his first set.

In the moment, my prediction didn't help him although it actually did me: acknowledging the inevitable somehow made me relax. In the past, I might have felt a surge of anxiety and the familiar race of adrenalin that could undo any semblance of control I might have had over my game. Now the inevitability of losing was calming and bittersweet: I could identify with Seth's approaching triumph, mourn the loss of my own and accept the passage of time fighting it all the way. That strengthened my resolve to win, not out of panic but from pride. Seth's turn would come soon enough and I wanted to hold on to mine as long as I could.

Not long afterward, Seth did win his first set from me. Then, the following week, after he and Josh had lost a semi-casual set of doubles to his father and me, they challenged us to a serious match, the best two out of three, losers each to pay $100. The boys went at it with dedication and ferocious pre-game fervor. Amidst much hype and strategic warfare, which included the silent treatment of my husband and me the morning of the match during breakfast and beyond, I still felt relaxed, actually curious about the outcome and amused by their efforts to psych me out. In my state of greater wisdom and self-knowledge, I was beyond that now, though I did note that they didn't bother directing their silence or later their quips toward my ever unflappable husband—only to me.

Although we tend to be extremely unceremonious about most things, we did up the occasion to suit the drama, with linesmen, pitchers of juice, and Seth's then-girlfriend Liz (now wife) and her then-dog Buck (now Thurman) perched on a rock to watch. I was playing well and staying relaxed even at my usual pressure points; if anything, my husband seemed to be making more errors than were usual for him. Could it be that my rock of Gibraltar was not as solid as I thought? Could he be having a touch of the jitters? His best shots were not working consistently (usually one of the best features of his game), a definite drawback since his steadiness on those occasions when we played doubles always tended to help me to settle down.

Nonetheless, we were playing well enough to take the first set to a tie-breaker, which the boys won.

In the second set, undaunted by the loss and reminding ourselves that first sets were really warm-ups, my husband and I were ahead 5-3, playing with more and more confidence, clearly holding our own. But as luck would have it, it was up to me to serve for the set. "Relax, it's only a game," I reminded myself, feeling every inch in control, a mature (and now well-psychoanalyzed player), but then proceeded to serve three double faults in a row. I wish I could say that, unfazed, I pulled myself together and went on to recover the game and with it, the set. Alas, not so.

It wasn't long before we lost the set and the match along with $100 to each of the boys amidst their shouts, guffaws, slap-me-fives, and all the magnificent outpourings of adolescent male triumph. Having literally not spoken to us since morning and full of the moment, they broke their silence, jumped over the net in unison (as if practiced until perfect) and offered us a rematch (with slight condescension) the following weekend—this time not for money but to confirm their superiority.

The next week my husband and I did better. We were up one set and ahead in the second with a score of five games to four when once again it fell to me to serve for the match. It was a drawn-out game with many ad points and even a familiar double fault—which immediately prompted the boys to redouble their teasing and efforts to provoke their mother-the-head-case to come through for them once again. This time however, amusement, experience, and even age won out and my husband and I took the match.

The psyche is a wondrous thing; I think I am learning to live with mine.

Author Biography

Fern W Cohen, Ph.D., a psychoanalyst and psychotherapist in private practice in New York City, has long been committed to conveying in everyday language what the psychoanalytic process is about and how it works. That passion informs her teaching and supervising as well as her writing, which includes her personal take on the professional problems raised by her experience with breast cancer **Stories of Illness and Healing: Women Write Their Bodies** *(Kent State University Press, in press 2007) and a prize-winning essay on the intersection of the prosaic and the professional ("Attachment is Where You Find It"). A graduate of Radcliffe College, Dr. Cohen earned her Ph.D. in School Psychology from New York University and completed her analytic training at the NYU Postdoctoral Program in Psychotherapy and Psychoanalysis as well as the Institute for Psychoanalytic Training and Research (IPTAR), of which she is a member.*

3871398

Made in the USA
Lexington, KY
02 December 2009